Intermediate to Advanced Piano Solo

THE WORLD'S GREAT CLASSICAL MUSIC

The Romantic Era

55 Selections from Symphonies, Ballets, Operas & Piano Literature
for Piano Solo

EDITED BY BLAKE NEELY AND RICHARD WALTERS

Cover Painting: Caspar David Friedrich, *The Chalk Cliffs of Rügen*, c. 1820

ISBN 978-0-634-04804

CORPORATION
7777 W. BLUEMOUND RD. P.O. BOX 13819 MILWAUKEE, WI 53213

Visit Hal Leonard Online at
www.halleonard.com

CONTENTS

Hector Berlioz   10   Symphonie Fantastique, Op. 14, Fifth Movement Excerpt
("Witches' Sabbath")

Alexander Borodin   14   Polovetzian Dances (from *Prince Igor*), First Theme

Johannes Brahms   20   Intermezzo in A Major, Op. 118, No. 2*
    17   Intermezzo in B-flat Major, Op. 76, No. 4*
    26   Lullaby (Wiegenlied)
    27   Rhapsody in G Minor, Op. 79, No. 2*
    36   Symphony No. 1 in C Minor, Op. 68,
       Fourth Movement Excerpt
    38   Symphony No. 4 in E Minor, Op. 98,
       First Movement Excerpt
    40   Waltz in A-flat Major, Op. 39, No. 15*

Anton Bruckner   47   Symphony No. 7 in E Major, Second Movement Excerpt

Fryderyk Chopin   50   Mazurka in A Minor, Op. 17, No. 4*
    56   Nocturne in C Minor, Op. 48, No. 1*
    62   Polonaise Militaire, Op. 40, No. 1*
    68   Prelude in D-flat Major, ("Raindrop"), Op. 28, No. 15*
    74   Waltz in A-flat Major, Op. 69, No. 1*

Antonín Dvořák   80   Slavonic Dance, Excerpt

Charles Gounod   42   Ave Maria ("Meditation") adapted from the
       Prelude in C by J.S. Bach
    84   Funeral March of a Marionette, Themes

Edvard Grieg   86   In the Hall of the Mountain King (from *Peer Gynt*)
    91   Morning (from *Peer Gynt*)

Franz Liszt   99   Liebestraum No. 3 in A-flat Major*

Gustav Mahler   96   Symphony No. 4 in G Major ("Ode to Heavenly Joy"),
       Third Movement Excerpt
    106   Symphony No. 5 in C-sharp Minor,
       Fourth Movement Excerpt
    110   Symphony No. 8 in E Major ("Symphony of a
       Thousand"), Second Movement Excerpt

Jules Massenet   115   Meditation (from *Thaïs*)

Felix Mendelssohn   118   "Fingal's Cave" Overture (The Hebrides), Themes
    120   A Midsummer Night's Dream, Overture Themes
    127   Symphony No. 4 in A Major ("Italian"), Op. 90,
       First Movement Excerpt

Modest Musorgsky   130   The Great Gate of Kiev (from *Pictures at an Exhibition*)*

Pieces originally for piano, the remaining works are piano transcriptions.

Jacques Offenbach	137	Barcarolle (from *The Tales of Hoffman*)
Sergei Rachmaninoff	140	Prelude in C-sharp Minor, Op. 3, No. 2*
Nicolay Rimsky-Korsakov	151	Sheherazade, Themes from Part 1
Franz Schubert	146	Andante (Second Movement) from Sonata in A Major, Op. 120*
	156	Ave Maria
	163	Impromptu in A-flat Major, Op. 142, No. 2*
	170	Moment Musicale in F Minor, Op. 94, No. 5*
	174	Symphony No. 8 in B Minor ("Unfinished"), First Movement Excerpt
	180	Symphony No. 9 in C Major ("The Great"), First Movement Excerpt
Robert Schumann	158	Piano Concerto in A Minor, First Movement Themes
	182	The Prophet Bird (Vogel als Prophet) from *Forest Scenes**
	186	Symphony No. 1 in B-flat Major ("Spring"), Op. 38, Third Movement Excerpt
	196	Widmung (Dedication)
Johann Strauss	191	By the Beautiful Blue Danube, Themes
	200	Tales from the Vienna Woods, Themes
Richard Strauss	203	Allerseelen (All Souls' Day)
	211	Also sprach Zarathustra!, Opening Theme
Pytor Il'yich Tchaikovsky	206	1812 Overture, Excerpt
	212	Dance of the Sugar Plum Fairy (from *The Nutcracker*)
	216	Piano Concerto No. 1 in B-flat Minor, Op. 23, First Movement Excerpt
	220	Romeo and Juliet Fantasy Overture, "Love Theme"
	224	Symphony No. 6 in B Minor ("Pathétique"), Op. 74, First Movement Excerpt
	238	Waltz (from *Swan Lake*)
	226	Waltz of the Flowers (from *The Nutcracker*), Excerpt
Richard Wagner	232	The Evening Star (from *Tannhäuser*)
	234	Pilgrims' Chorus (from *Tannhäuser*)

ABOUT THE COMPOSERS...

HECTOR BERLIOZ (1803-1869).

Credited as the inventor of the modern orchestra, Hector Berlioz was one of the most original, creative composers of his age. He used phrases of irregular lengths, striking rhythms and inventive, colorful combinations of orchestral instruments to create new sounds using the traditional orchestral instrumentation. Although hailed today as the greatest French composer of the Romantic era, Berlioz was condemned during his lifetime as eccentric or simply wrong. Even as a young man, he managed to win the Prix de Rome on his fourth attempt — only by tempering his composition to follow a traditional style that would please the judges. As a child, Berlioz studied the flute and guitar. Following his father's wishes, he entered medical school, but after two years decided to follow his own career aspirations rather than his father's plans for his future. As a result, his father cut off financial support, leaving the young composer struggling for several years. Berlioz's career was a constant struggle for acceptance. In addition to composition he worked as a music critic and as a conductor. Berlioz was tremendously influenced by literary works, particularly by Shakespeare. Among his greatest orchestral works are *Symphonie fantastique, Harold en Italie* and *Roméo et Juliette*. Now hailed as the greatest of his five operas, *Les Troyens* (The Trojans) was not performed in French, in its complete version, until 1969. Although *Les Troyens* is not as long as the lengthier works of Wagner, and despite the fact that Berlioz intended it to be heard in a single performance, the opera is often split over two evenings when performed. Berlioz's eventual slide into depression and illness was exacerbated by the loss of his father, his two wives and his son as well as a number of friends. He became preoccupied with death, by some accounts longing to die. His music was not to be fully understood or appreciated until the twentieth century.

ALEXANDER BORODIN (1833-1887).

Alexander Borodin's success as a composer is astounding in the light of his double life. Borodin was a member of the Moguchaya Kuchka (Mighty Handful, or Mighty Five), a group of the five great Russian nationalist composers that included Balakirev, Borodin, Cui, Musorgsky and Rimsky-Korsakov. His works were known internationally during his lifetime and the "Polovetsian Dances," from his opera *Prince Igor,* remains a favorite in the classical repertoire today. The other side of Borodin's double life was an enormously successful career in medicine. As a child the composer taught himself the cello while pursuing a fascination with science. As an adult, his musical interests were always secondary to his research and lecturing. He taught at the Medico-Surgical Academy in St. Petersburg, traveling throughout Europe to give papers and lectures. Borodin allied himself with the Russian nationalists, making use of Russian folk songs and folk melodies in his works. He first achieved international recognition as a composer with *On the Steppes of Central Asia*. In addition to three symphonies, chamber music and vocal pieces, Borodin wrote five operas during his lifetime. Of the five, he completed only one, *Bogatïri* (The Bogatïrs). His greatest work was the opera *Prince Igor,* on which he worked from 1869 through 1887. Unfinished at the time of his death, the work was completed and partially orchestrated by Glazunov and Rimsky-Korsakov. Although it is based on Borodin's own libretto, which has been called weak and disjointed, the opera contains a great deal of remarkable music.

JOHANNES BRAHMS (1833-1897).

Johannes Brahms was a man of strong opinions. He disapproved of the "New German School" of composers, namely Liszt and Wagner. He avoided what he believed to be the excesses of the tone poem, relying instead on traditional symphonic forms. After his Symphony No. 1 was premiered, he was hailed as "Beethoven's true heir." The symphony, written when Brahms was forty-three years old, is so clearly linked to the symphonies of Beethoven that it is jokingly been called "Beethoven's Tenth." Brahms began his musical studies as a youngster, gaining experience in composition and working as an arranger for his father's light orchestra. He revered composer Robert Schumann. On the advice of Franz Liszt he met Schumann, with whom he developed a close friendship. He also developed a deep love for Schumann's wife Clara Wieck Schumann. From the time of Schumann's mental breakdown until his death in 1856, Brahms and Clara tended to the ailing composer. The truth of the relationship between Brahms and Clara Schumann remains something of a mystery. Brahms never married. Clara Schumann never re-married following Robert's death. When Clara Schumann died in May of 1896, Brahms did not get to the funeral due to a missed train connection. He died the following April. Throughout his life, Brahms would sign letters "Frei aber froh" (Free but happy), until his last years when he signed "Frei aber einsam," (Free but lonely). One of the pall-bearers at Brahms' funeral was the composer Antonín Dvořák.

ANTON BRUCKNER (1824-1896).

Austrian composer and organist Anton Bruckner was one of the more controversial figures of the Romantic era. An unwitting musical revolutionary, he came of age as a composer in an era during which the concert-going public was deeply divided between the music of Brahms and the music of Wagner. He and his music were caught up in the public war between followers of the two great composers. Much of his music was not fully appreciated by international audiences until years after his death. Bruckner was a deeply religious man from humble beginnings. He was middle-aged by the time he arrived in Vienna, sporting country manners, dress and accent, and possessing virtually no social sophistication. He retained his dress and customs, and never grew comfortable in Viennese society. Part of Bruckner's social naiveté stemmed from his many years in a monastery. He was enrolled as a monastery chorister at 13, following his father's death, and later taught at the same monastery for ten years. He left the monastery at 31, when he won the post of cathedral organist in the city of Linz. In the ten years he spent in Linz, Bruckner was exposed to the music of Wagner, which broke many of the rules of composition that he had been taught, but achieved a musical level to which he aspired. Although he became a revolutionary in his own way, he never saw himself in this light. He broke musical ground by taking Wagner's use of descriptive themes and harmonic freedom to new levels. When he was 44 he accepted a professorship at the Vienna Conservatory, where he would spend the rest of his life. Throughout his life, Bruckner was plagued by bouts of depression, shyness and a very poor opinion of himself. The harsh criticism lobbed at him from the Brahmsians hurt him deeply.

FRYDERYK CHOPIN (1810-1849).

Although composer and pianist Fryderyk Chopin was born to a French father and spent half of his life in Paris, he always defined himself by the land of his birth, Poland. Throughout his life he retained strong nationalistic feelings. Chopin the pianist achieved the status of an idol. His mystique was based in part on his cultured upbringing and in part on his fragile good looks. His sensitive nature, frail health, and self-imposed exile only intensified the public's fascination with him. In 1831, after receiving his training and achieving some success in Poland, Chopin moved to Paris. There he found himself one of many piano virtuosos. Although he quickly made a name for himself, his temperament and physical frailty, caused by tuberculosis that plagued him throughout much of his life, left him poorly suited to life as a performer. He gave only about 30 performances, many of which were private affairs. From 1838 to 1847 Chopin was romantically involved with novelist Georges Sand (Aurore Dudevant). The years of their stormy romance were his most productive as a composer. While Franz Liszt created works of grand proportions and brilliant virtuosity, Chopin remained a miniaturist, creating elegant, fluid melodies within the framework of small pieces. He was the only great composer who wrote almost exclusively for the piano. Chopin is set apart from other Romantic era composers by the fact that his works were not inspired by or based upon literature, works of art, or political ideals. Composition was difficult work for Chopin, who was a gifted improviser from his earliest days. He composed as he played, finding it painful to commit his work to paper. When Chopin and Georges Sand parted ways in 1847, the composer's frail health took a turn for the worse. He was further weakened by his 1848 concert tour of England. When he died in October of 1849, public fascination only increased, as evidenced by the nearly 3,000 mourners who attended his funeral.

ANTONÍN DVOŘÁK (1841-1904).

Antonín Dvořák's parents were firm believers that a child must learn to play an instrument and sing. Dvořák's father, an innkeeper by trade, was an avid amateur musician who played in the town band in Bohemia. But a career in music was unthinkable. The young Dvořák was expected to follow in his father's trade. After many battles the young musician was finally allowed to enter music school. After finishing his studies he took a job in an opera orchestra, taking on private students as well. By his mid-thirties he was supporting himself in great part with his compositions. Brahms, who later became his friend, helped him find a publisher for his work. His fame gradually spread throughout Europe and from there to the United States. In 1885 Dvořák was invited to become director of the National Conservatory of Music in New York City. In his homeland, Dvořák had been both a fan and a student of folk music. In America he delightedly found a new style of folk music to study. He was particularly taken with the African-American spiritual. Yet he was homesick while in New York. Eventually he found a small Bohemian settlement in Spillville, Iowa, where he could spend his summers speaking his native tongue and generally relaxing in familiar cultural surroundings. In Spillville he worked on his Symphony No. 9, "From the New World." It was premiered in New York in 1893 and was a huge success. In 1895 homesickness took Dvořák back to Prague, where he became director of the Prague Conservatory. He continued to compose, but the disastrous premiere of his opera *Armida* in March of 1904 hurt him deeply. Two months later he died suddenly while eating dinner.

CHARLES GOUNOD (1818-1893).

While French composer Charles Gounod was in Rome competing for the Prix de Rome, which he won on his third try in 1839, he discovered sixteenth-century polyphonic music wafting about the Sistine Chapel. He was so moved by this music, and likely by the setting as well, that he considered becoming a priest. Instead, he began composing masses and worked as a church organist in Paris. When he began writing operas, he leaned heavily on the examples of Gluck and Meyerbeer. Although these first operas were failures, he soon found his own voice, creating the likes of *Roméo et Juliette* and *Faust*. With *Faust* he struck a blow for French composers. *Faust*, although not a resounding success at the outset, was a powerful opera that came from the pen of a Frenchman. The opera put a dent in the domination of foreign operas in Paris and opened doors for other aspiring French composers. In the fifty years that followed, *Faust* was performed some two thousand times in Paris alone. It was the opera that opened the new Metropolitan Opera Company in New York in 1883. Gounod weathered the Franco-Prussian war living in England, becoming the first conductor of the Royal Albert Hall Choral Society. He returned to Paris in 1875, where he continued to work on operas. From 1881 to the end of his life he wrote almost exclusively church music. Like Mozart, he began a requiem that would prove to be his own. He was sitting at the piano, working on the Requiem, when he slumped onto the keyboard. He died three days later. Gounod's "Funeral March of a Marionette," written in 1873, is best known to television audiences as the Alfred Hitchcock theme.

EDVARD GRIEG (1843-1907).

Edvard Grieg holds a unique position in music history as not just the most famous of Norwegian composers, but as one of the only Norwegian composers to have achieved an international reputation. Grieg drew upon traditional Norwegian folk songs for the inspiration and basis for many of his pieces. His incorporation of national folk music into classical forms inspired musicians throughout Europe to do the same with the traditional music of their own countries. Although Grieg's Piano Concerto in A Minor is his best known work, it is not typical of his style. Most of his pieces are small in scale, giving him a reputation as a miniaturist. Grieg's first music lessons came from his mother. When Norwegian violinist Ole Bull heard the teen-aged Grieg play the piano, he arranged for him to enter the Leipzig Conservatory in Germany. Although the young musician was terribly homesick, living so far from home, he enjoyed the opportunity to hear performances by such luminaries as Clara Schumann and Richard Wagner. After his studies in Germany, and later in Denmark, Grieg returned to Norway. Finding himself in demand throughout Europe, Grieg spent much of his career traveling. The recipient of honorary degrees from Cambridge and Oxford, Grieg was also honored as one of his country's foremost composers.

FRANZ LISZT (1811-1886).

Critics of the Hungarian composer/pianist Franz Liszt, the most famous pianist in history, accused him of composing music that was little more than a vehicle for self-promotion. He was the greatest pianist of his age, and judging from accounts of his playing and the music he composed for himself, he may have been the greatest pianist who has ever lived. His limitless piano technique set a standard for concert pianists that remains in effect to this day. Liszt was a larger-than-life character who generously supported the work of other composers and single-handedly invented the modern piano recital. His romantic life was legendary. He lived for many years with the Countess Marie D'Agoult, although she was married to another man. Liszt fathered two children with the Countess (one of whom would later marry conductor Hans von Bülow, only to leave him for composer Richard Wagner). Liszt later entered a romance with Princess Carloyne Sayn-Wittgenstein, for whom he left the concert stage and became Kapellmeister to the Grand Duke of Weimar. For a decade he lived in Weimar, writing and refining much of the music for which he is known. In his later years he took minor orders in the Roman Catholic church. Liszt was a generous teacher and taught a large number of students, exerting a profound influence over music-making in Europe for decades. He was also a conductor, and lead premieres of new works by Wagner, Berlioz and Verdi. As a composer Liszt looked to the future. His melodrama, "Der träurige Mönch," an atonal composition based on a tone row, clearly foreshadowed the subsequent work (decades later) of Arnold Schönberg. Public fascination with Lizst, the most famous celebrity in Europe, continued throughout his life. Not long before he died he celebrated his seventy-fifth birthday by embarking on a Jubilee tour that received press coverage around the world.

GUSTAV MAHLER (1860-1911).

Gustav Mahler was not exactly a musician's musician. His perfectionism caused him to alienate many of the musicians with whom he worked. When he became music director of the Vienna Royal Opera he cleaned house, replacing orchestral singers and orchestral musicians. He restaged existing productions, seeing to every detail of the productions himself. The musicians considered him heavy-handed, while the opera's management felt he was spending money wildly. Mahler was a workaholic. He devoted his summers to composition since his conducting schedule during the concert season was non-stop. As a composer he devoted his energy entirely to songs, song cycles and symphonies. The symphonies are enormous, involved, Romantic works. They were brutally treated by the critics of his day. His symphonies did not find receptive audiences until after World War II, when they found unprecedented success. Mahler left the Vienna Royal Opera, sailing for New York to conduct at the Metropolitan Opera. While in New York he became instrumental in the revitalization of the New York Philharmonic. But his inability to slow down was taking its toll. Mahler had been warned that his heart was weak and was told to cut back on his working hours. Cutting back was impossible. He worked at his usual feverish pace until he collapsed in New York on February 21, 1911. Unable to return to work, he was moved to Paris for treatments. When it became apparent that he would not recover, he asked to be moved to Vienna where he died on May 18, 1911. The story has been told that in his last hours he conducted an imaginary orchestra with a single finger. It has also been said that his last word was "Mozart."

JULES MASSENET (1842-1912).

On the way to becoming one of the most popular French composers of the latter nineteenth century, Massenet taught himself the art of orchestration by playing percussion at the Paris Opera. He struck financial success composing a series of operas based on subject matter that mixed romance and religion, culminating in his 1894 opera, *Thaïs*. His most famous operas, *Manon*, in 1884, and *Werther*, in 1892, put him at the helm of French opera for the next twenty years. A young American soprano, Sibyl Sanderson, greatly admired by the composer, premiered the role of Manon and later sang the role of Thaïs. Massenet continued to write twenty more operas, outpacing his rivals in the genre. Massenet followed the footsteps of Charles Gounod using a similarly sentimental melodic style that won him the nickname 'daughter of Gounod.' He consciously restricted his style to the tastes of the affluent Parisians, a quality that disgusted some of his envious contemporaries, like Debussy, who sought more intellect and less suavity and charm in their musical sound. However, as an unselfish, life-long teacher at the Paris Conservatory, Massenet made a lasting influence on new French composers, thus laying the foundation for stylistic departures. Massenet continued to write operas into the early twentieth century with works like *Le jongleur de Notre-Dame*, 1902, a medieval Christmas tale. It was about this same time that Debussy began to emerge and surpass Massenet as the most important French opera composer.

FELIX MENDELSSOHN (1809-1847).

While most of Mendelssohn's colleagues could tell stories of their battles with family over choice of career and even more tales of their financial struggles as musicians, Felix Mendelssohn could only listen. He was born into a wealthy family that supported his goals in music from the very first. Even in their conversion from Judaism to Christianity, which the family had long considered, they were spurred to action by thoughts of their son's future. It was at the time of their conversion that they changed the family surname to Mendelssohn-Bartholdy. Mendelssohn set out on his musical career with two clear goals. He wanted to re-introduce the largely forgotten music of old masters such as Bach to the public, and he dreamed of opening a first-rate conservatory. At the age of twenty he conducted a pioneering performance of Bach's *St. Matthew Passion*, the first of many such concerts he would lead. A few years later he founded and directed the Leipzig Conservatory. As a composer, Mendelssohn combined the expressive ideals of the Romantics with the traditional forms of the Classical era. He is remembered both as one of the great Romantic composers and one of the last of classicists. In his career Mendelssohn found success at an early age, and remained highly successful until his death. His sister Fanny, to whom he was exceptionally close, died suddenly on May 14, 1847. Shortly after he got the news of his sister's death, Mendelssohn fell unconscious, having burst a blood vessel in his head. Although he recovered from this incident, he was terribly diminished by the illness. His health and mental state deteriorated until his death on November 4 that same year. Memorial services for the great conductor/composer were held in most German cities, as well as in various cities in Great Britain, where he had become quite a celebrity.

MODEST MUSORGSKY (1839-1881).

Son of a prosperous landowner, Modest Musorgsky was one of the most original Russian composers in history. His life would change from that of a young, sharp-looking officer to a prematurely aged, ravaged man living in abject poverty. Modest took piano lessons at an early age, improvising music already without much training. He studied composition with Balakirev at age nineteen. The early German romantics influenced Musorgsky, but his visit to Moscow in 1858 fortified his beliefs in a strong Russian national spirit. Settling largely in St. Petersburg, he held military and ministerial offices while struggling to find time and energy to compose. It is perhaps the more roughshod, amateur musical training and inborn abilities that he relied on that marked him as a true original, so differently from his more professionally trained contemporaries, Borodin, Balakirev, Cui and Rimsky-Korsakov. He had written only experimental operatic fragments before eventually completing his magnum opus, *Boris Godunov*, a strikingly original opera based on a story of a Russian czar. Because of the opera's politically charged subject matter, any full production of the opera was banned by the imperial theaters. A company of singers, however, defiantly mounted a performance benefit of a few scenes that generated success and an eventual production. In 1873 he endured the sudden loss of one of his friends, Victor Hartmann, a watercolorist, architect designer and stage designer. A memorial exhibition of the artist's work was displayed. The various drawings and sketches inspired Musorgsky to compose perhaps his most famous piece, *Pictures at an Exhibition*, a colorful cycle of piano pieces featuring a recurring promenade theme and short movements that depict several of Hartmann's drawings. A long history of alcoholism and various ailments eventually took Musorgsky's life at age forty-two.

JACQUES OFFENBACH (1819-1880).

One of the finest tune-smiths of the nineteenth century, Jacques Offenbach helped define the genre of operetta. The international popularity of his operettas paved the way for the creations of such composers as Franz Lehár, Victor Herbert and the team of Gilbert and Sullivan. The operettas of Offenbach and others formed the roots of twentieth-century musical theater. Offenbach was raised in France, although his family was German in origin. He began his musical life with studies on the violin, switching to cello at a young age. Although his comic operas were a tremendous success both in France and abroad during the 1860s, the French civil war of 1870-71 triggered a change in musical taste. Following the war, Offenbach's operettas were no longer the rage they had once been. In 1876, in an effort to make some much needed money, Offenbach embarked on a tour of the United States. He played some forty concerts in the U.S., writing a book on his impressions of America upon his return to France. At the time of his death, Offenbach had completed 95 operettas and comic operas. He also wrote numerous vocal pieces and works for cello, as well as five ballets, additional dance music, vaudevilles and incidental music. Many of his operettas contain sharply witty lyrics that are punctuated by fairly blatant musical effects. Two of Offenbach's operas were unfinished at the time of his death: *Belle Lurette* was completed by Delibes, while his one serious opera, *Les Contes d'Hoffmann* (The Tales of Hoffmann), was completed by Guiraud. *Les Contes d'Hoffmann* is considered his masterpiece, still popular with opera companies throughout the world today.

SERGEI RACHMANINOFF (1873-1943).

Once described by composer Igor Stravinsky as "a six-and-a-half-foot-tall scowl," Sergei Rachmaninoff's stern visage was a trademark of sorts. Rachmaninoff first found fame as a pianist, touring throughout his native Russia to critical acclaim. His compositions won notice in those early years as well, including a Moscow Conservatory Gold Medal in composition. Yet the 1897 premiere of his Symphony No. 1 was a complete failure, due in large part to poor conducting by Alexander Glazunov. The dismal reception of the piece sent Rachmaninoff into a three-year creative slump that he overcame through hypnosis. During those three years he began conducting, earning international respect for his work on the podium. When his Symphony No. 1 received its London premiere in 1909, it was a huge success. Rachmaninoff made his first U.S. tour in 1909. On the tour he featured his Piano Concerto No. 3, which he had written expressly for his American audiences. Rachmaninoff fled Russia in the wake of the October Revolution of 1917. He brought his family to America where he continued to concertize, but did not compose for nearly a decade. After years of touring, Rachmaninoff decided that the 1942-43 concert season would have to be his last. In January of 1943 he began to suffer from an illness diagnosed as pleurisy. He gave what was to be his final performance on February 17. He then returned to his Beverly Hills home where he died of cancer on March 28.

NIKOLAY RIMSKY-KORSAKOV (1844-1908).

Trained as an officer in the Russian Navy, composer Rimsky-Korsakov had a great interest in music but little training beyond piano lessons. Although he displayed prodigious talents as a child, his aristocratic standing meant that a career in music was out of the question. Yet, after teaching himself counterpoint and harmony, and establishing himself as a composer, he became a professor at the St. Petersburg Conservatory. He was removed from that position when he publicly condemned the police control over the school and its students. Among his students were Alexander Glazunov and Igor Stravinsky. He is remembered as the central figure of "The Russian Five" (or "The Mighty Five"), a group of composers that included Modest Musorgsky, Alexander Borodin, César Cui and Mily Balakirev. The group favored a dynamic national style in distinct contrast to the elegant sounds of Tchaikovsky. Rimsky-Korsakov composed more than fifteen operas, numerous choral works and orchestral pieces, a great quantity of vocal music, as well as chamber works and piano pieces. Of this great quantity of music only three orchestral pieces have remained in the classical repertoire: the symphonic suite *Sheherazade* for which he is best remembered, his *Spanish Capriccio* and his *Russian Easter Festival*. Written in 1888, *Sheherazade* is based on vignettes from "Tales of the Arabian Nights."

FRANZ SCHUBERT (1797-1828).

The story of Schubert's life reads like a heartbreaking novel. Now hailed as one of the great Romantic composers, not one of Schubert's symphonies was performed during his lifetime. It was five decades after his death before any of them were published. Schubert, the son of a school headmaster, was not a virtuoso musician. Although his musical abilities were readily apparent to his teachers, his inability to perform left him with little means to support himself. He taught in his father's school for a time, but was miserable in that job. Schubert studied with Salieri, who was astounded by the young composer's abilities. After writing his first symphony at age fifteen, Schubert presented Salieri with a completed, fully orchestrated opera two years later. Schubert lived less than thirty-two years, yet he composed a phenomenal amount of music, including some six hundred songs. One hundred and forty-four of those songs date from the year 1815, a year in which he was teaching at his father's school. After Schubert left his father's school, he had the good fortune to collect a small group of devoted friends and supporters. The friends would periodically organize evenings of the composer's music, which came to be known as "Schubertiades." Schubert's health began to fail as early as 1822. When he died, at age thirty-one, he was viewed as a composer of songs. It was not the enormous number of songs that earned him this mistaken designation so much as the fact that almost none of his other music had been performed during his lifetime. In addition to the songs, Schubert completed seven symphonies, and left one unfinished. He wrote a number of operas, although these are far from his best works. He also wrote choral works, chamber music and piano pieces. In accordance with his dying wish, he was buried beside Beethoven, whom he had idolized and at whose funeral he served as a torch-bearer.

ROBERT SCHUMANN (1810-1856).

Robert Schumann's dream was to become a pianist. As the son of a German bookseller and writer, he grew up surrounded by literature and instilled with a love of music. His world crumbled however, when he was just sixteen, with the death of his father and the subsequent suicide of his sister. Schumann entered law school, but spent most of his time studying music. In 1830 he moved into the household of his piano teacher, Friedrich Wieck. Soon afterwards, his left hand began to trouble him. His career dreams were shattered when his left hand became permanently crippled. He turned his energies to composition, making a name as a music critic as well. An inspired critic, he founded the music journal *Neue Zeitschrift für Musik*, in 1834. He often wrote under the pseudonyms "Florestan" and "Eusebius." Schumann fell in love with with his teacher's daughter, Clara Wieck, a highly acclaimed concert pianist. Clara's father fought vigorously against the romance. Schumann married Clara in 1840, but only after he had taken his case to the courts. In the year he was married, the composer wrote some 150 songs, turning to orchestral music the following year. Schumann suffered from bouts of terrible depression, which became progressively worse with time. In 1854 he attempted suicide. Unable to function any longer, he was then placed in an asylum, where he spent the last two years of his life. His wife and his friend, the young composer Johannes Brahms, looked after him in those final years.

JOHANN STRAUSS, JR. (1825-1899).

Just as John Philip Sousa was America's March King, Johann Strauss Jr. was Austria's Waltz King. The Strauss family is synonymous with the waltz. Johann, Sr. was a violinist, conductor and composer, who was widely popular throughout Europe. He conducted in a flamboyant style, with violin in hand. He popularized the open-air concert and programmed many of his numerous works. His son Josef was also a conductor, working with the family orchestra and composing a number of pieces as well. Eduard, a younger son, became Vienna's imperial-royal music director from 1872-1901. He was the most respected conductor of the Strauss clan, and was in great demand throughout Europe. But it was Johann, Jr. who won the hearts of the Austrian people. His talent was recognized early and his first composition was published when he was only six years old. As an adult, he formed a rival orchestra to his father's and began to tour with his own music. Eventually the two groups were merged into a single family orchestra. While the public loved Johann, Jr., the world of classical music saw him as lacking substance. For all the criticism he received during his lifetime, his music is familiar to classical audiences a century after his death. During Johann, Jr.'s last days, the city of Vienna waited anxiously for hopeful news of his health. On June 3, 1899, a large crowd gathered for an outdoor concert. In mid performance, a messenger bolted onto the stage and whispered something into the conductor's ear. The conductor abruptly stopped the orchestra. After a few moments they began playing the opening notes of "By the Beautiful Blue Danube," Strauss' beloved waltz. The audience knew in an instant what it meant. Their Strauss had died. Rising to their feet, the men removed their hats and bowed their heads while women cried. A few days later, Johann Strauss, Jr.'s obituary referred to him as "the last symbol of cheerful, pleasant times."

RICHARD STRAUSS (1864-1949).

The eighty-five years of Richard Strauss' life straddled two centuries, included two world wars and saw radical changes in the world of classical music. When the German composer was born, Wagner was at work on his opera *Siegfried,* Brahms was years away from beginning his Symphony No. 1 and Debussy was a toddler. By the time Strauss died, with Europe in post-World War II shambles, tonal music seemed a thing of the past and composers of traditional symphonic sounds were finding themselves relegated to the writing of film scores. Yet even in the last years of his life, Strauss held to Romantic musical values that had fallen out of fashion years earlier. He had earned a reputation as Germany's most exciting composer with orchestral pieces such as *Don Juan* and *Salome* in 1905. In 1909, his opera *Elektra* pushed the limits of propriety and shocked audiences with its immoral story. Just when it seemed as though he would step into the atonal writing of many of his contemporaries, he introduced his opera *Der Rosenkavalier,* an elegant, lyrical comedy. In 1933 Strauss was forced to step out of his idyllic, mountain villa in Garmisch to face a harsh reality. The Nazis had appointed him President of the Reichsmusikkammer, a post that made him the national representative of German music. He held the post for two years, continuing with his own compositions on the side. When the Nazis demanded that Strauss denounce his Jewish librettist and friend, Stefan Zweig, he refused and was removed from his official position. He stayed in Germany, tolerated by the Nazis due to his international fame. His continued presence ensured the safety of his Jewish daughter-in-law. Strauss was the source of controversy throughout the music world for much of his career. His music shocked audiences with its subject matter, while his unwillingness to abandon Romantic ideals kept the critics writing. On his first trip to the U.S., he performed in the rather unorthodox setting of a large drapery store. When critics attacked these inartistic circumstances, he replied that the situation made the concerts more of an artistic event than those in traditional venues. Always prone to sarcasm, he added that it was better to make money honestly than to complain about those who don't. Following World War II, Strauss retired to his mountain home, where he died shortly after his eighty-fifth birthday. Strauss' *Also Sprach Zarathustra* became familiar to a wide audience when it was heard in the soundtrack of the film *2001: A Space Odyssey.*

PYOTR IL'YICH TCHAIKOVSKY (1840-1893).

It is a curious twist of fate that the composer of so bombastic a work as the *1812 Overture* should have been an extremely fragile individual. Exceptionally sensitive from childhood, Tchaikovsky eventually deteriorated into a precarious emotional state. Tchaikovsky's musical abilities were already quite evident by age five, as was his hypersensitivity. His mother died when he was fourteen, a painful event that some say prompted him to compose. Over the years he was plagued by sexual scandals and episodes we might call "nervous breakdowns" today. Historians have uncovered evidence that his death, which was officially listed as having been caused by cholera, was actually a suicide. Many believe that the composer knowingly drank water tainted with cholera. Tchaikovsky's work stands as some of the most essentially Russian music in the classical repertoire, yet he was not a part of the Russian nationalistic school. In fact he was treated quite cruelly by critics of his day. "Tchaikovsky's Piano Concerto No. 1, like the first pancake, is a flop," wrote a St. Petersburg critic in 1875. A Boston critic claimed that his Symphony No. 6 ("Pathétique") "...threads all the foul ditches and sewers of human despair; it is as unclean as music can well be." For all the vehement criticism the composer received during his lifetime, his works are now among the best loved of the classical repertoire. His ballet *The Nutcracker* is an international holiday classic, while *Swan Lake* is staple in the repertoire of ballet companies throughout the world. His *1812 Overture* is among the most recognizable of all classical pieces. In 1893 the composer completed work on his Symphony No. 6. The first movement dealt with themes of passion, the second with romance, the third with disillusionment and the finale with death. The piece was premiered on October 28. Nine days later the composer was dead.

RICHARD WAGNER (1813-1883).

Wagner must be considered one of the greatest musical icons of the nineteenth century whose music continues to be idolized to this day. He had many influential ideas concerning the unification of music, drama, poetry, and art, as well as innovations in expansive orchestration, chromatic harmony, and a new kind of powerful singing. Wagner's contemporaries and those composers that followed in the latter nineteenth century and early twentieth century had to come to terms with his controversial music, either choosing to embrace it, or to deliberately part from its ways. As a student Richard was inspired by the nine Beethoven symphonies, while his schoolwork suffered in the name of music. He began as an opera composer and chorus master in Prague, then soon conducting other operas in the repertory. Always a revolutionary, he involved himself in the 1848 political uprisings in Paris and Dresden, and had to flee to Switzerland, aided by the famous pianist and friend, Franz Liszt. Money was always an issue for Richard, often writing to Liszt of his financial straits. He was constantly seeking funds for performances of his works, as well as cash for the construction of his newly designed opera house in Bayreuth, which featured his invented orchestral pit, which sat underneath the stage. Another ambitious project was his completion of an operatic quadrilogy, *Der Ring des Nibelungen* (The Ring Cycle) that was intended to be performed in the opera house over a course of several evenings. It took him twenty-six years to complete it, with interruptions between operas to write other large works. The composer also wrote his own librettos for his operas, drawing from Norse mythology and medieval subjects. His musical industry and extensive writings were evidence of his complete artistic focus and egocentric character (and add to that a colorful life filled with love affairs and marital crises.) He wrote, "I know nothing of the real enjoyment of life... my heart has had to move to my head and my living become artificial; it is only as the 'artist' that I can live."

Symphonie Fantastique
Fifth Movement Excerpt, "Witches' Sabbath"

Hector Berlioz
1803-1869
Op. 14
originally for orchestra

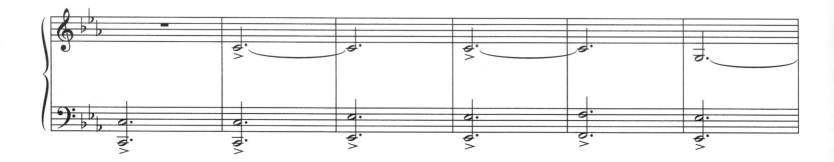

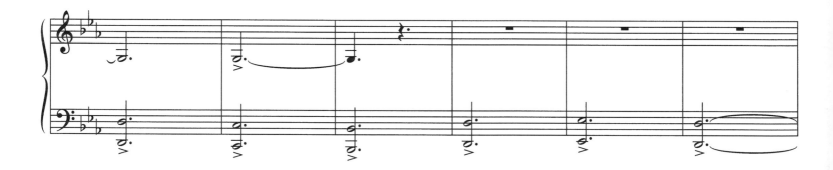

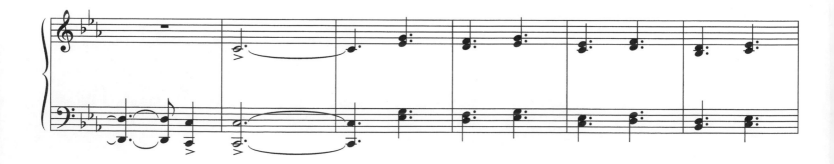

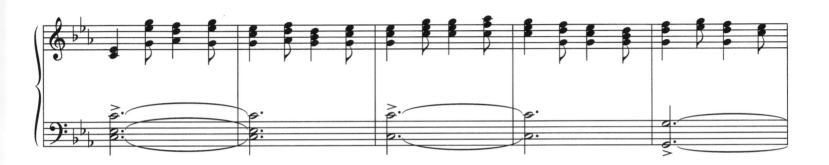

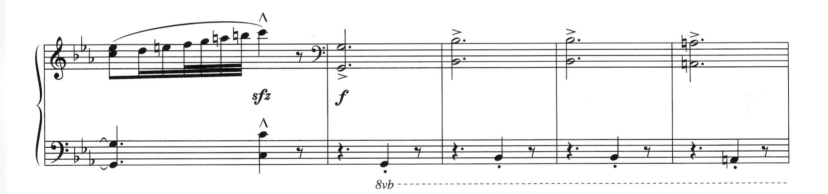

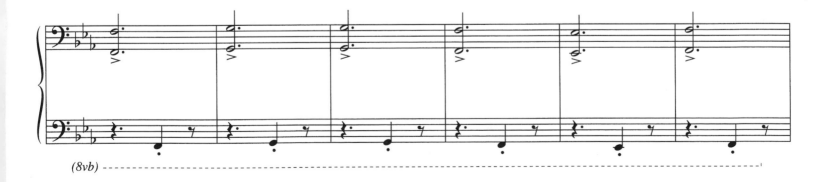

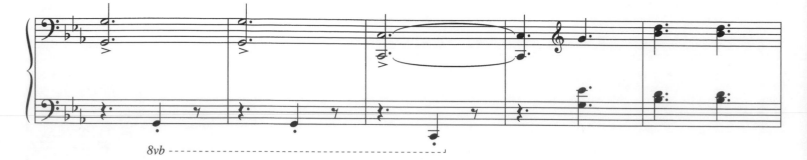

8vb- -

sfz

f

8vb- -

(8vb)- -

Polovetzian Dances

from the opera PRINCE IGOR
First Theme

Alexander Borodin
1833-1887
originally for orchestra

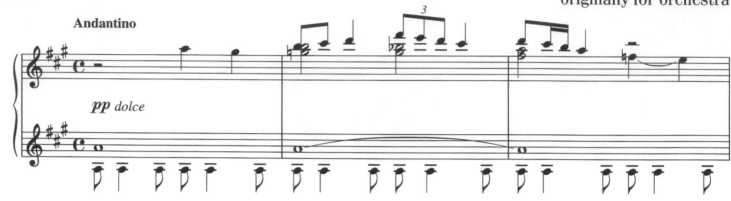

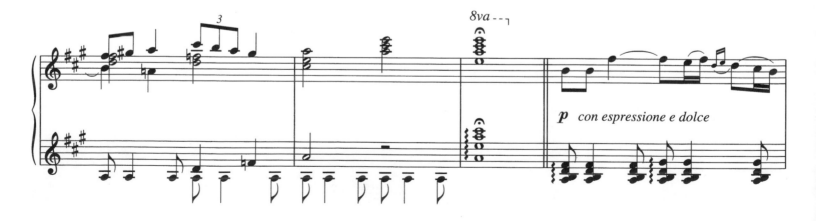

Intermezzo in B-flat Major

Johannes Brahms
1833-1897
Op. 76, No. 4

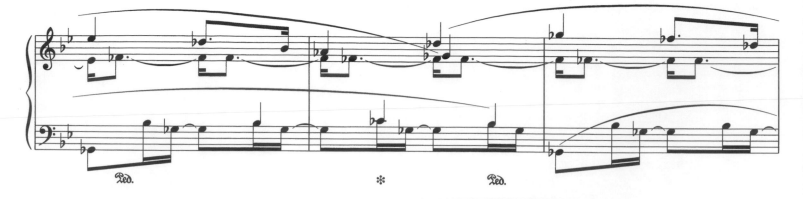

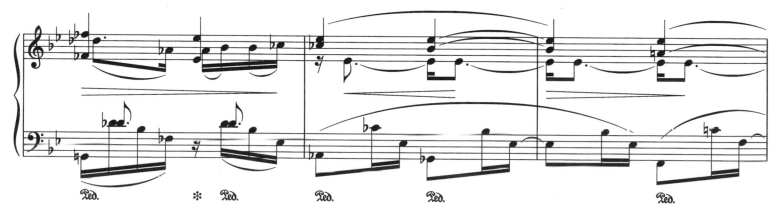

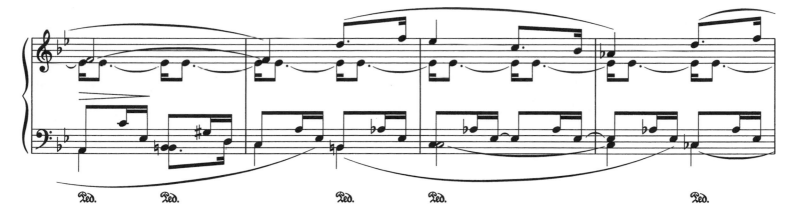

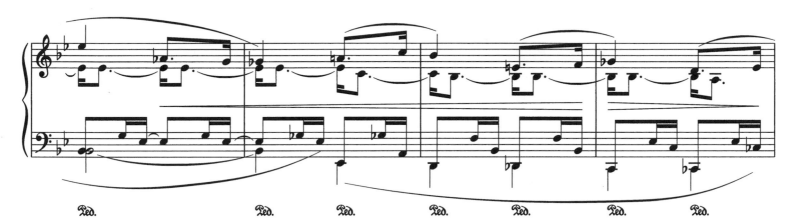

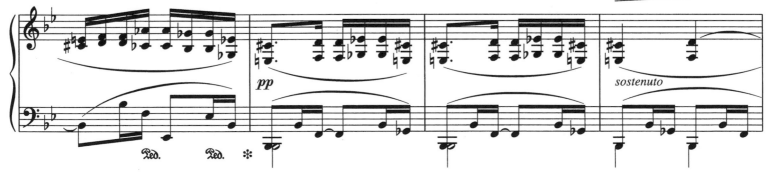

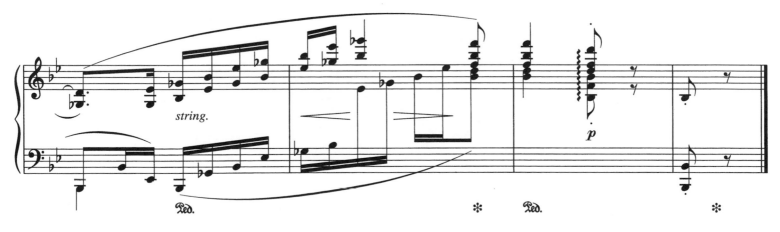

Intermezzo in A Major

Johannes Brahms
1833–1897
Op. 118, No. 2

Andante teneramente

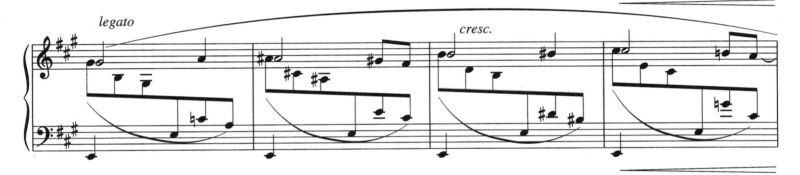

cresc., un poco animato

più lento

rit.

p

p

a tempo

3

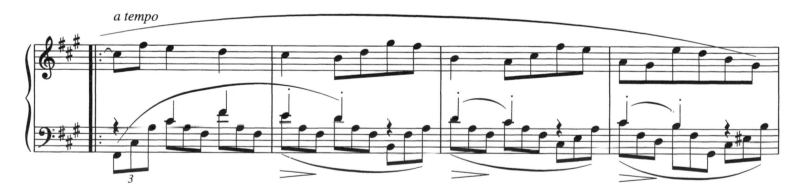

rit.

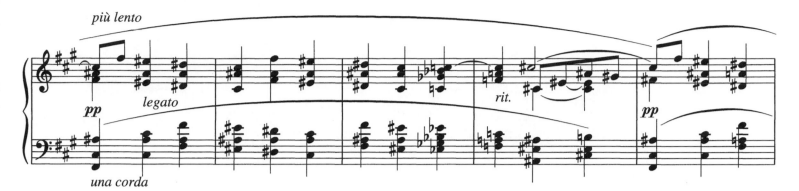

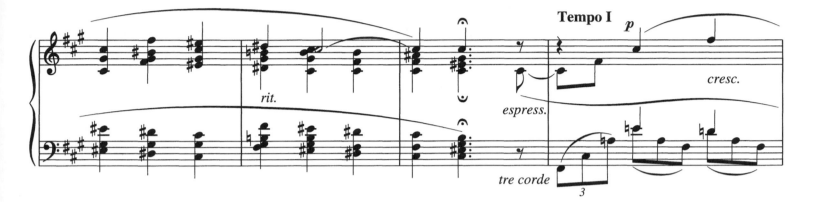

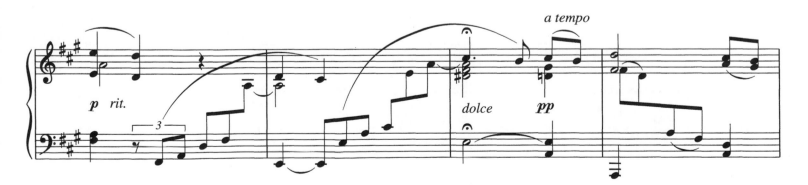

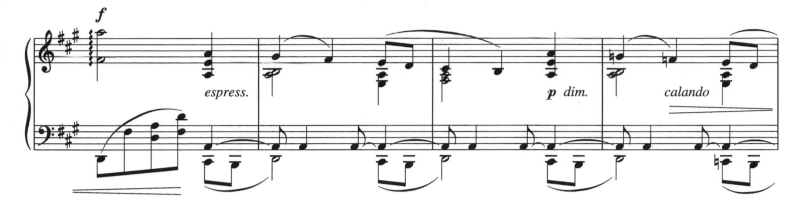

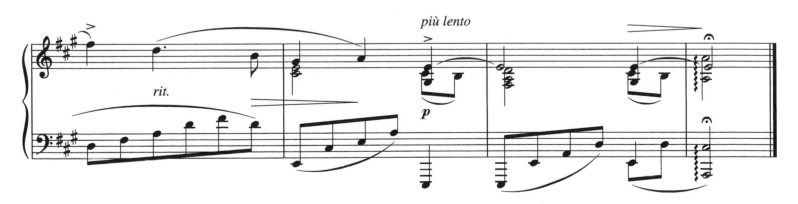

Lullaby
(Wiegenlied)

Johannes Brahms
1830-1897
Op. 49, No. 4
originally for voice and piano

Rhapsody in G Minor

Johannes Brahms
1833–1897
Op. 79, No. 2

Molto passionato, ma non troppo Allegro

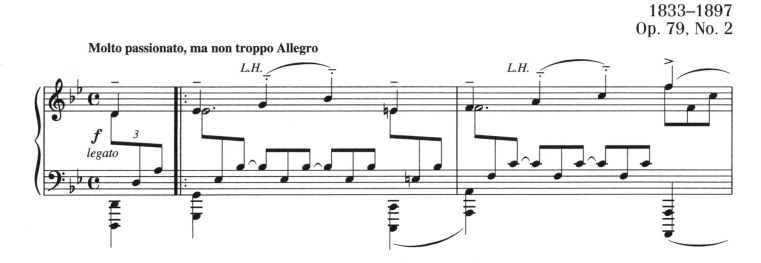

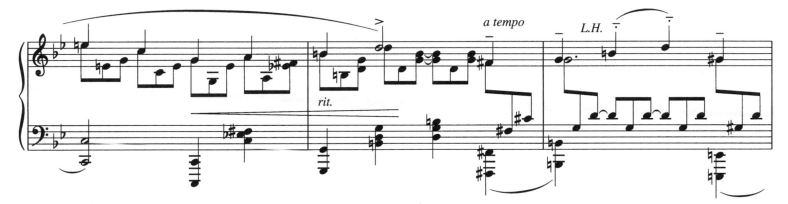

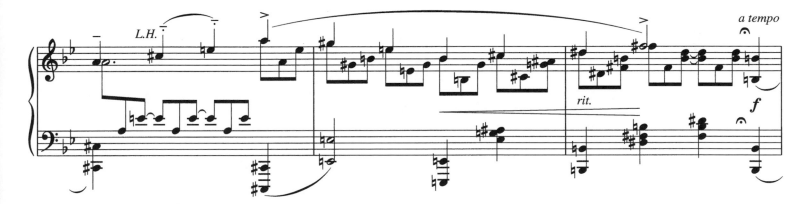

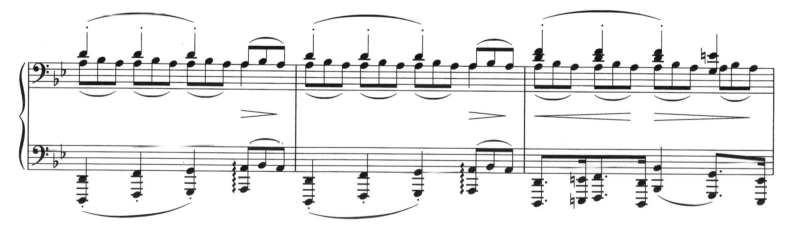

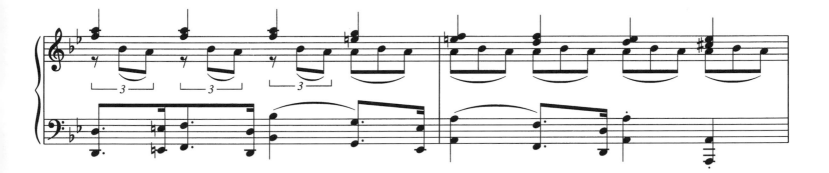

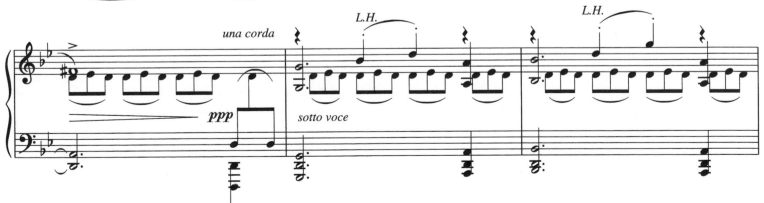

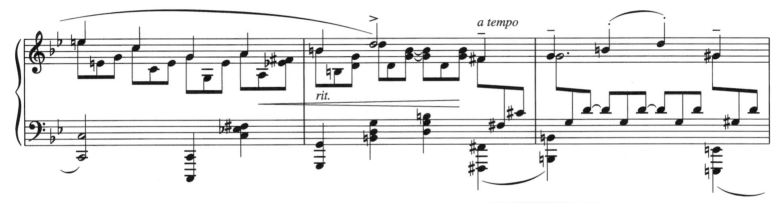

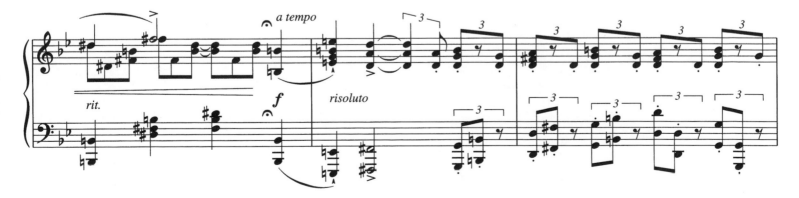

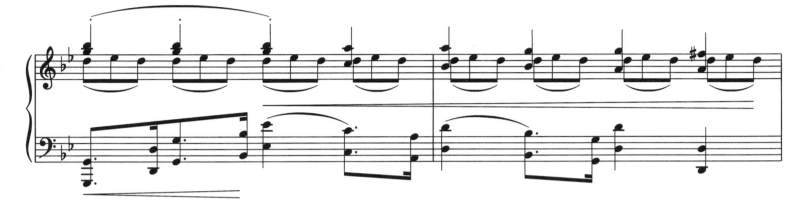

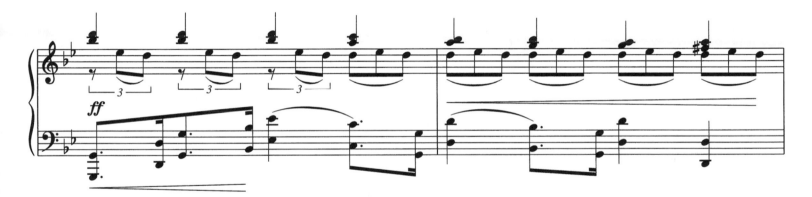

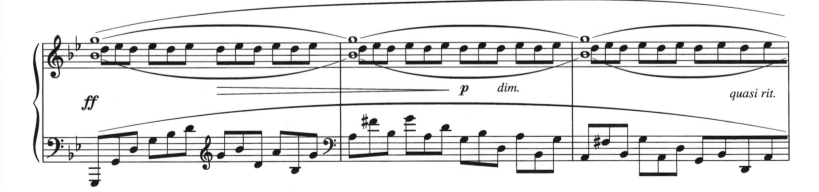

Symphony No. 1 in C Minor
Fourth Movement Excerpt

Johannes Brahms
1830-1897
Op. 68
originally for orchestra

Allegro non troppo ma con brio

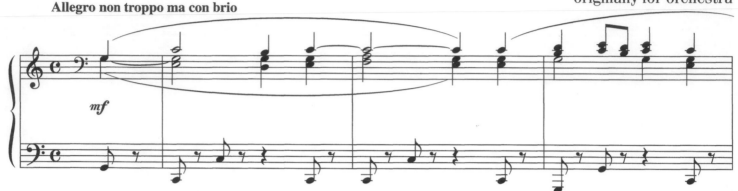

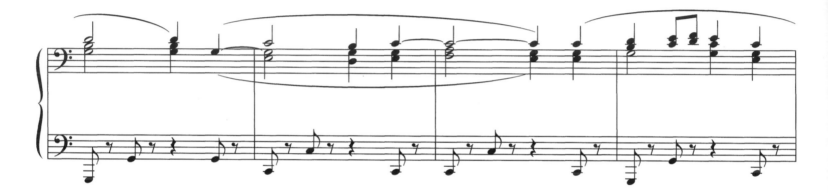

Symphony No. 4 in E Minor

First Movement Excerpt

Johannes Brahms
1830-1897
Op. 98
originally for orchestra

Waltz in A-flat Major

Johannes Brahms
1833-1897
Op. 39, No. 15

Ave Maria

"Meditation"
adapted from the Prelude in C by J.S. Bach

Charles Gounod
1818-1893
originally for chamber ensemble

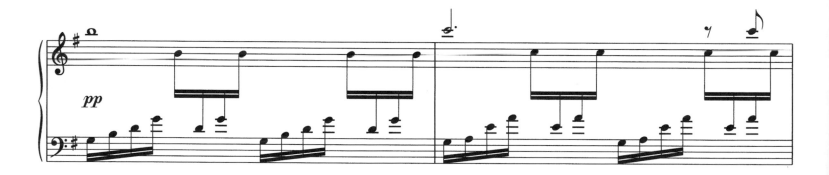

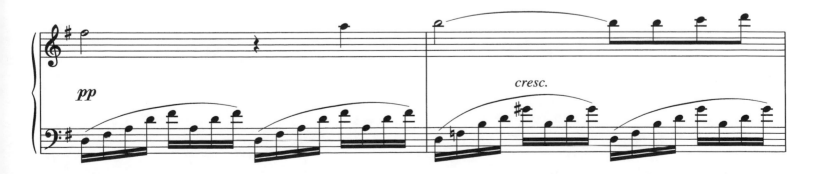

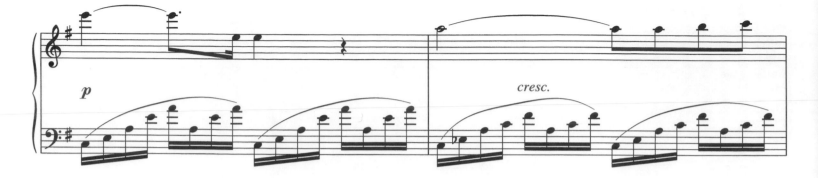

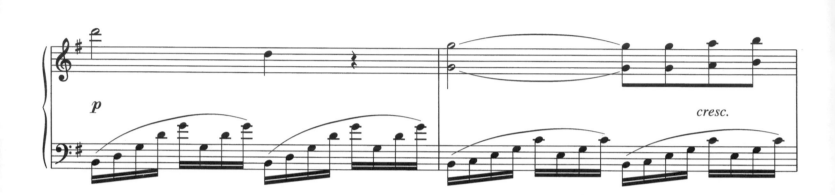

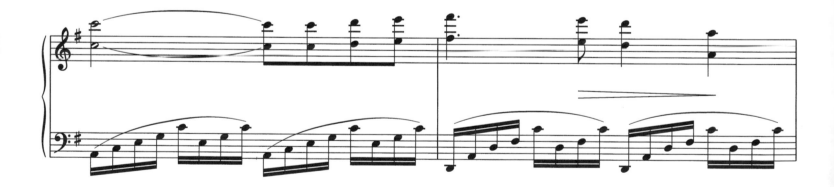

Symphony No. 7 in E Major
Second Movement Excerpt

Anton Bruckner
1824-1896
originally for orchestra

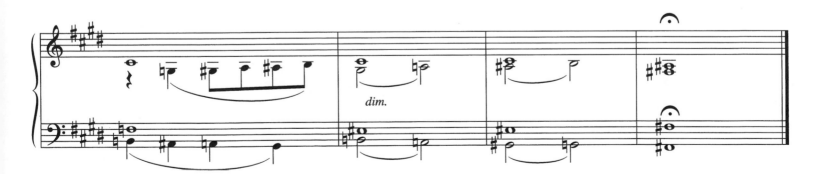

Mazurka in A Minor

Fryderyk Chopin
1810–1849
Op. 17, No. 4

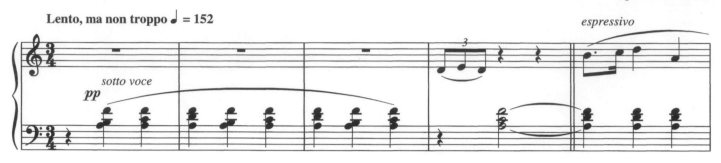

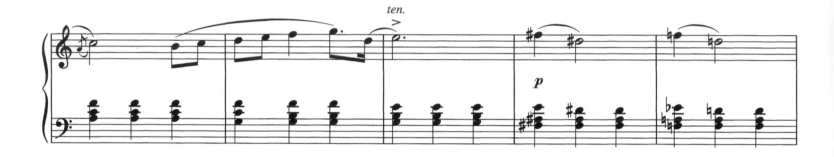

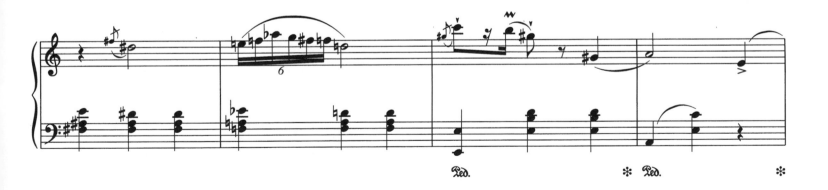

sotto voce

sempre più piano

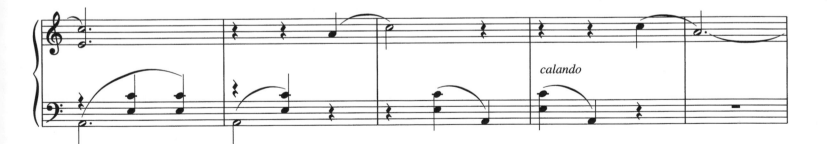

calando

perdendosi

Nocturne in C Minor

Fryderyk Chopin
1810–1849
Op. 48, No. 1

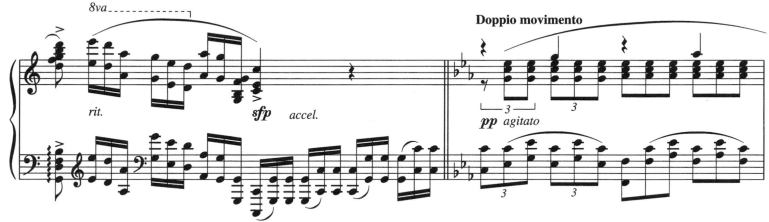

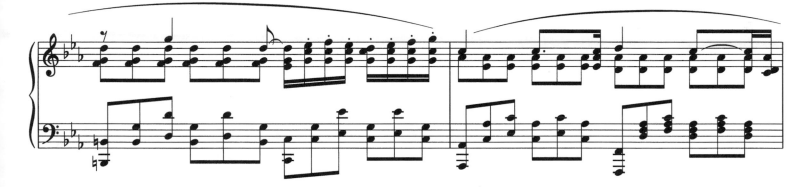

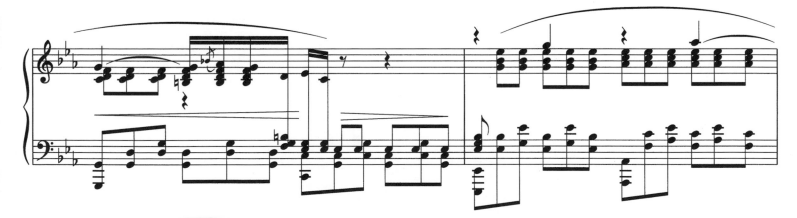

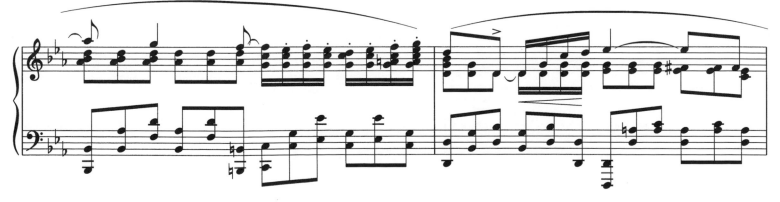

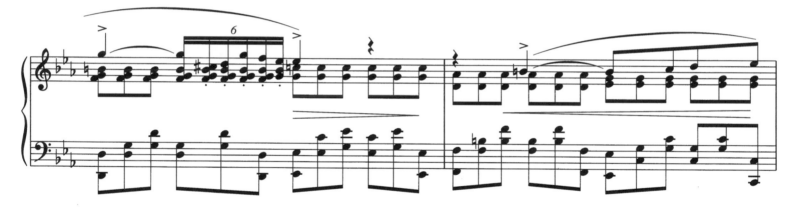

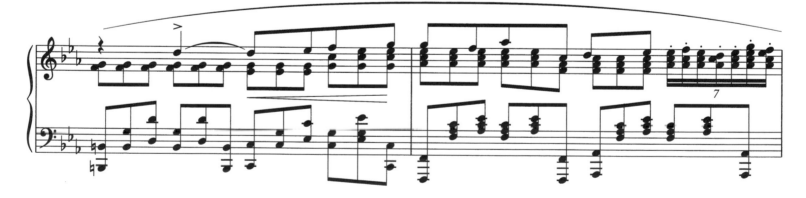

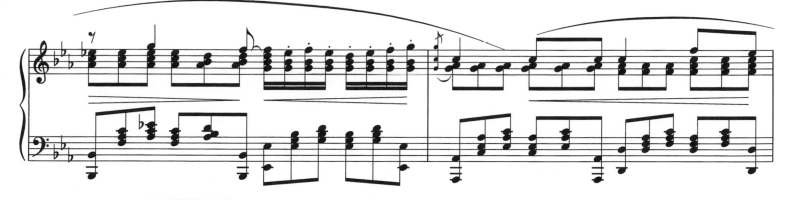

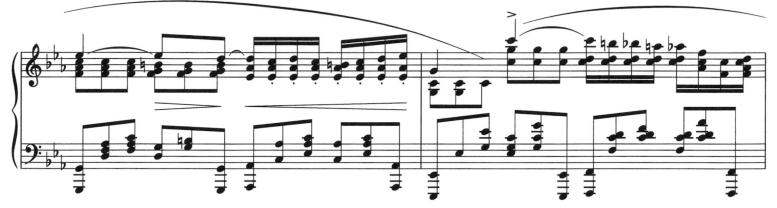

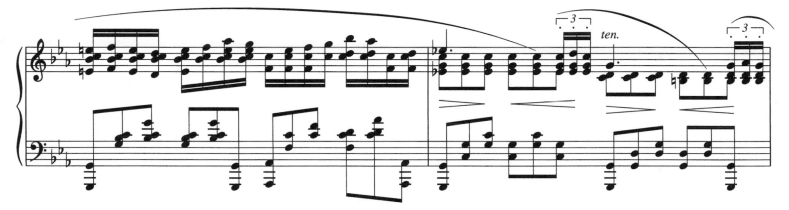

Polonaise Militaire

Fryderyk Chopin
1810–1849
Op. 40, No. 1

Allegro con brio

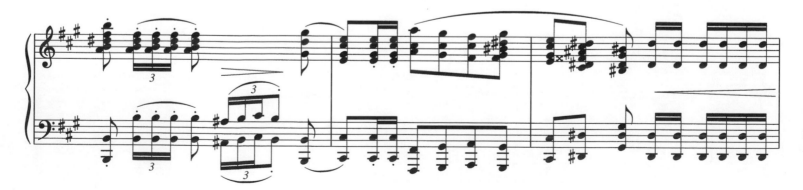

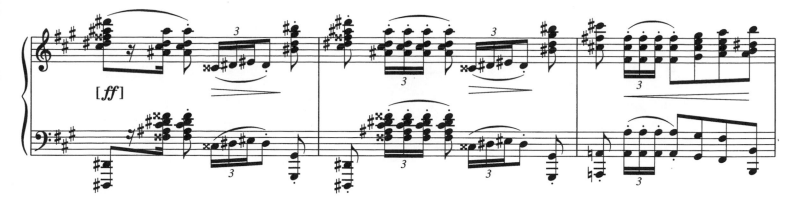

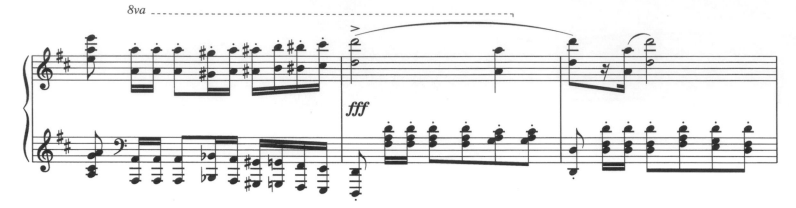

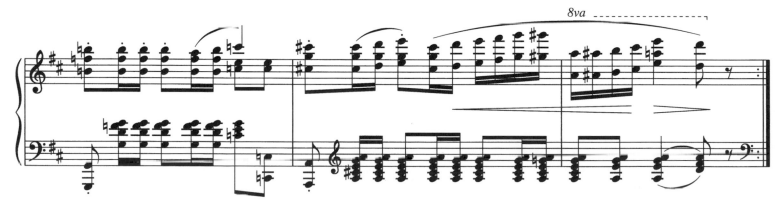

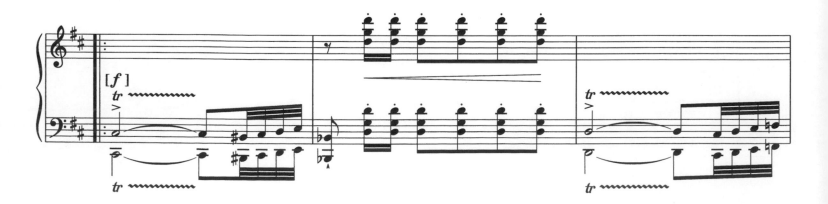

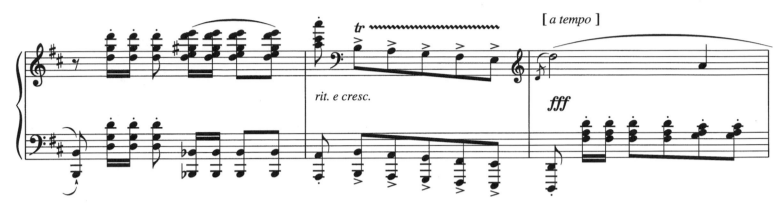

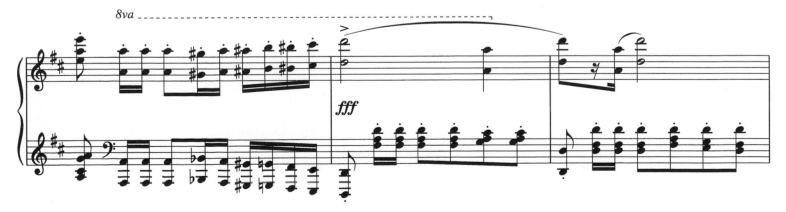

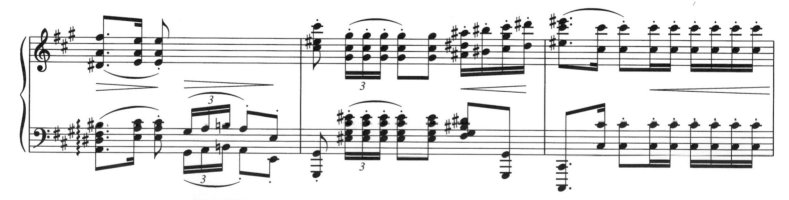

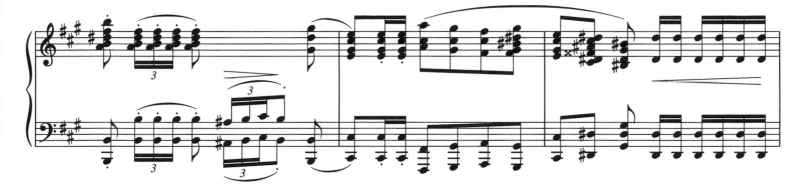

Prelude in D-flat Major
("Raindrop")

Fryderyk Chopin
1810-1849
Op. 28, No. 15

Sostenuto

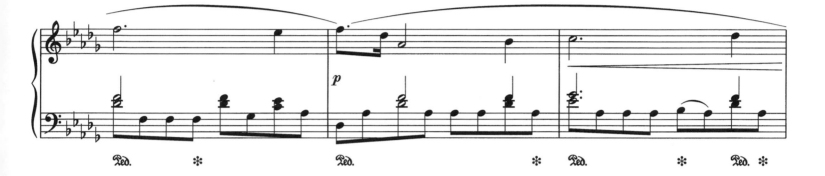

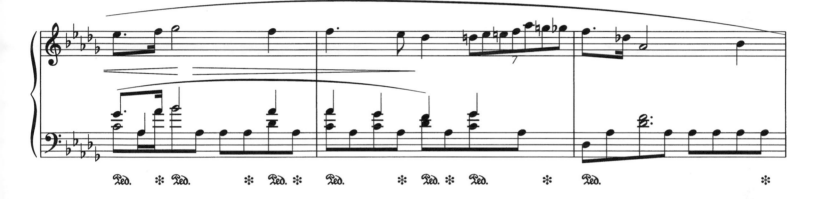

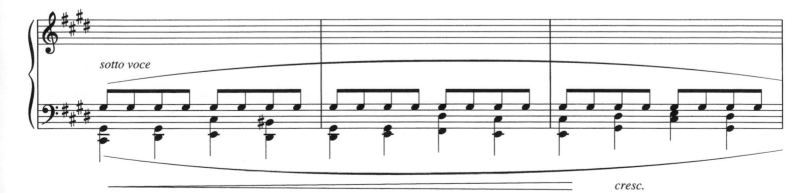

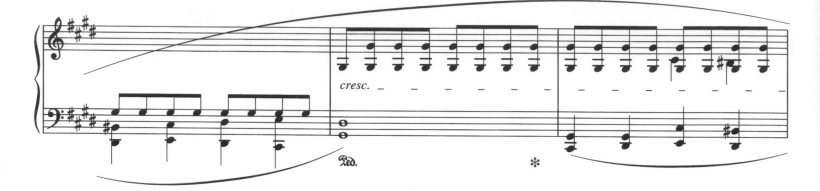

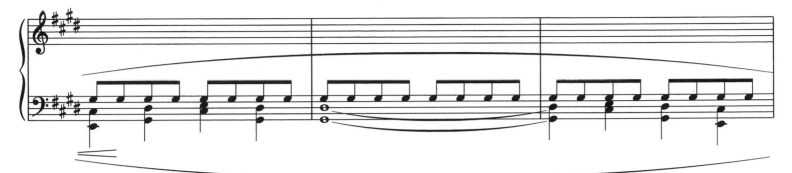

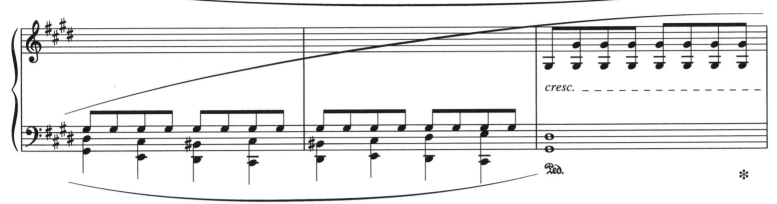

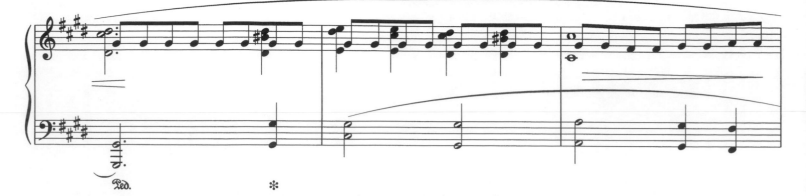

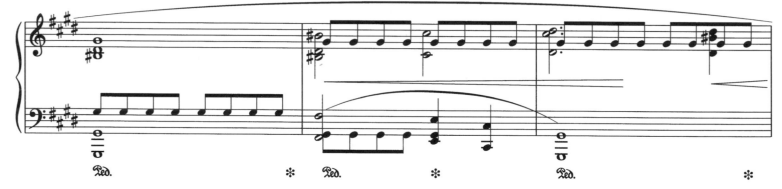

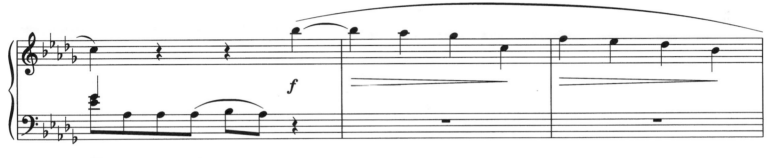

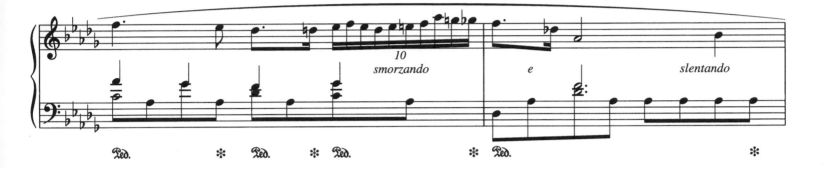

Waltz in A-flat Major

Fryderyk Chopin
1810-1849
Op. 69, No. 1

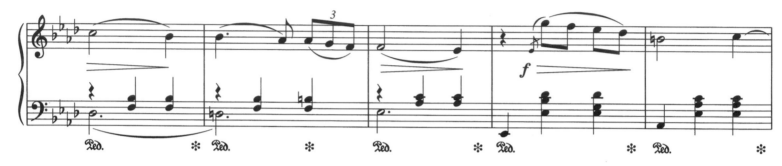

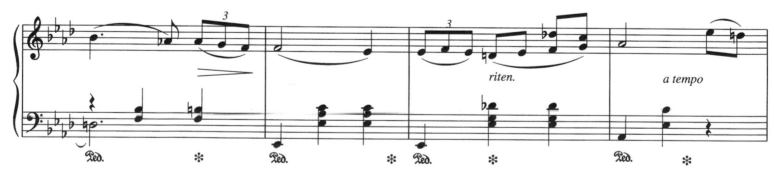

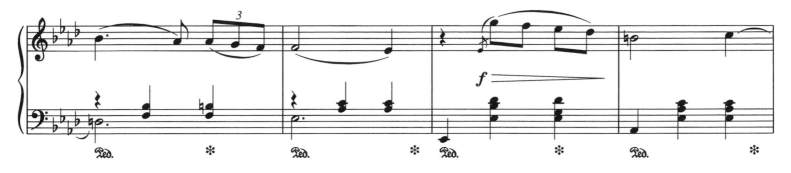

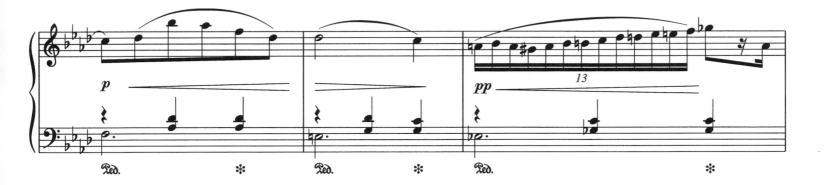

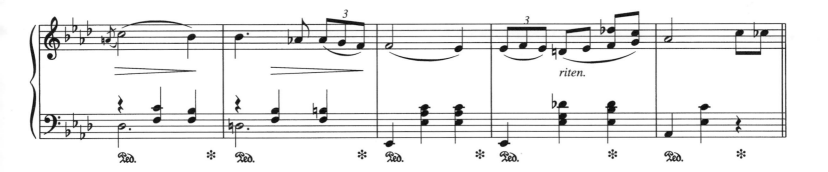

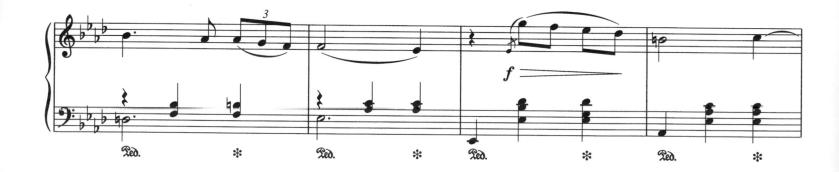

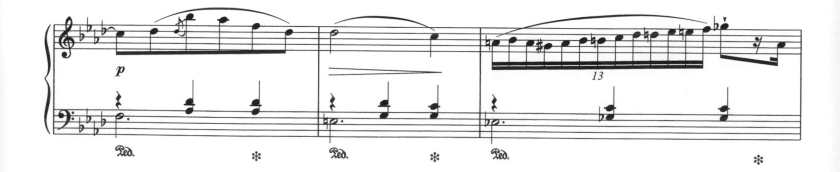

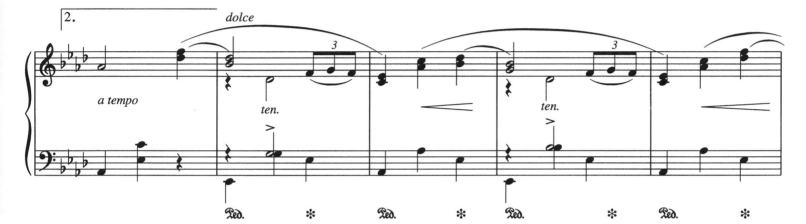

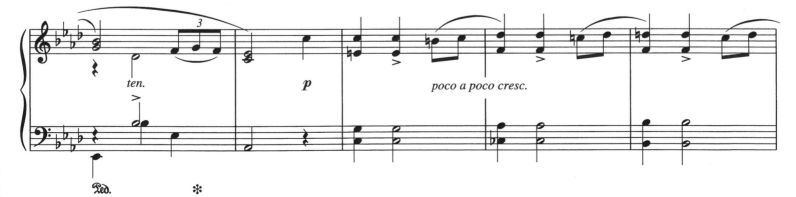

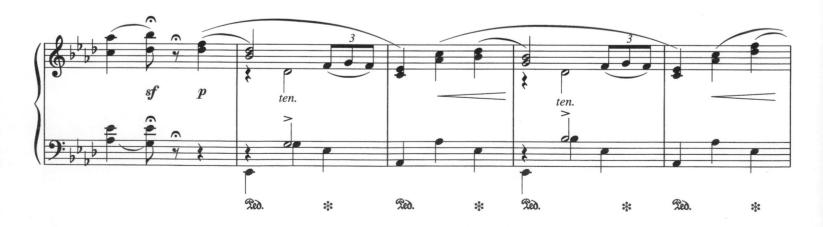

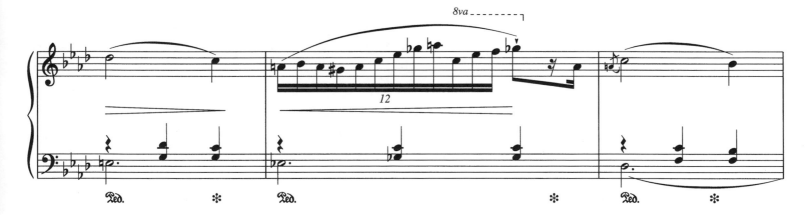

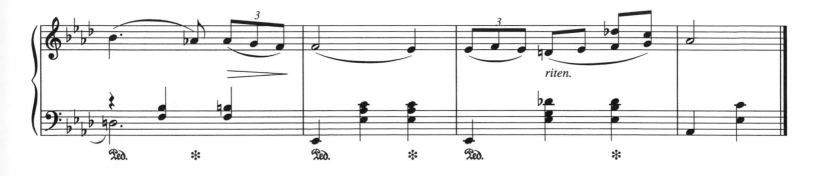

Slavonic Dance
Excerpt

Antonín Dvorák
1841-1904
Op. 46, No. 1
originally for piano, four hands
orchestrated by the composer

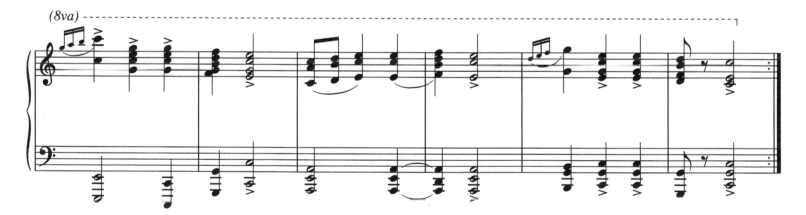

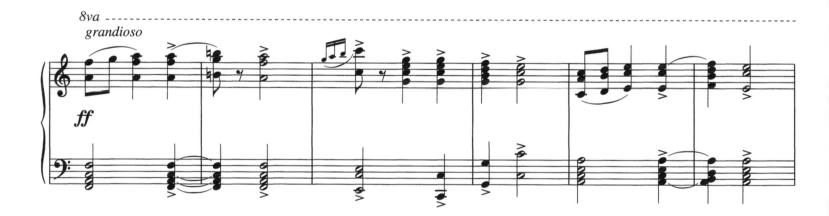

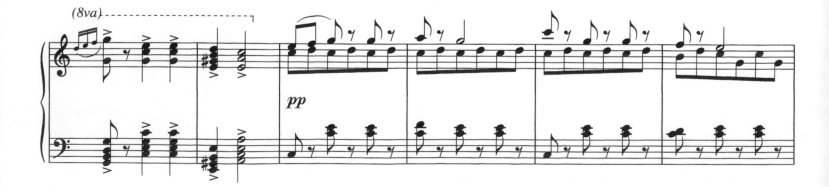

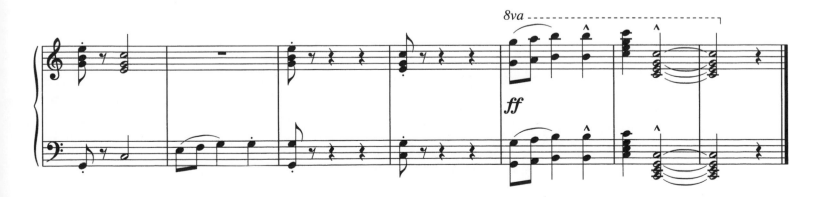

Funeral March of a Marionette

Themes

Charles Gounod
1818-1893
originally for orchestra

Allegretto

In the Hall of the Mountain King

from PEER GYNT

Edvard Grieg
1843-1907
Op. 23, No. 7
originally for orchestra

Alla marcia e molto marcato

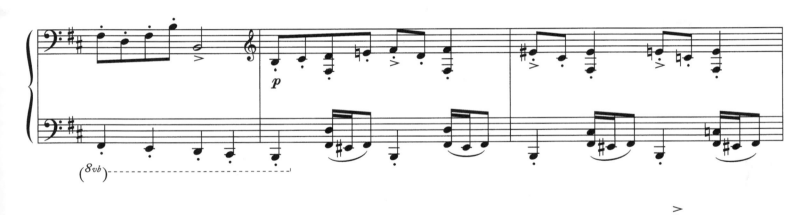

poco a poco cresc. e stretto

mf *e sempre cresc.*

Morning
from PEER GYNT

Edvard Grieg
1843-1907
Op. 23, No. 13
originally for orchestra

Allegretto pastorale

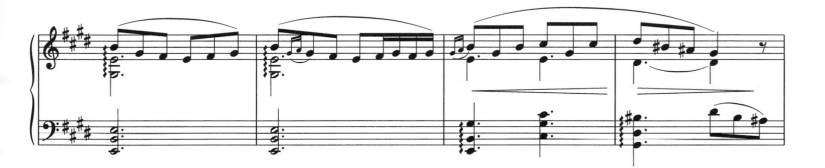

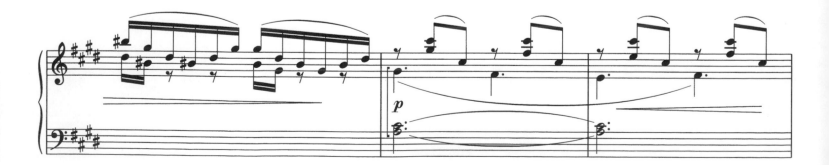

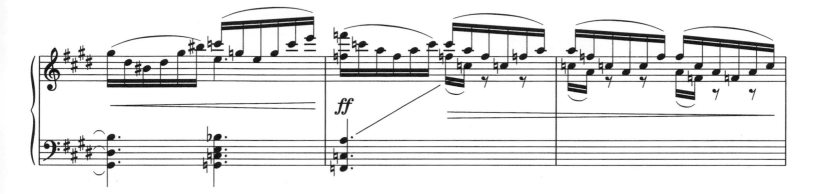

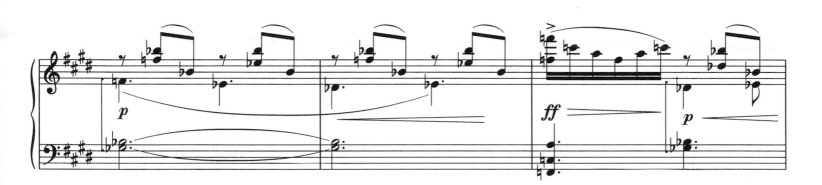

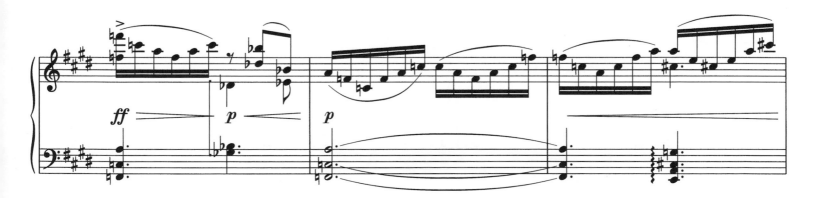

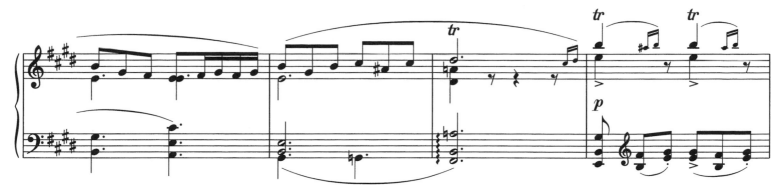

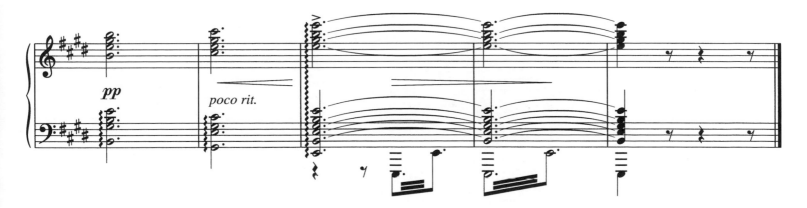

Symphony No. 4 in G Major

"Ode to Heavenly Joy"
Third Movement Excerpt

Gustav Mahler
1860-1911
originally for soprano and orchestra

Poco adagio

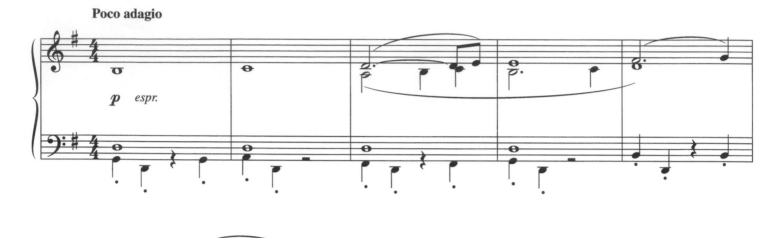

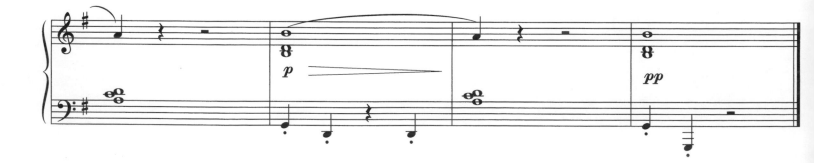

Liebestraum No. 3 in A-flat Major
(Nocturne No. 3)

Franz Liszt
1811–1886

Poco allegro, con affetto

dolce cantando

poco cresc. ed agitato

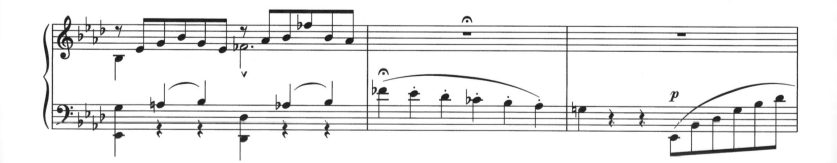

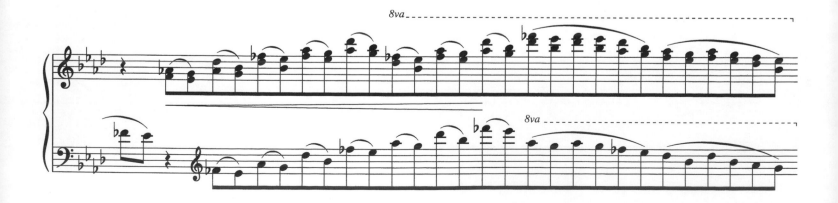

più animato, con passione

sempre string.

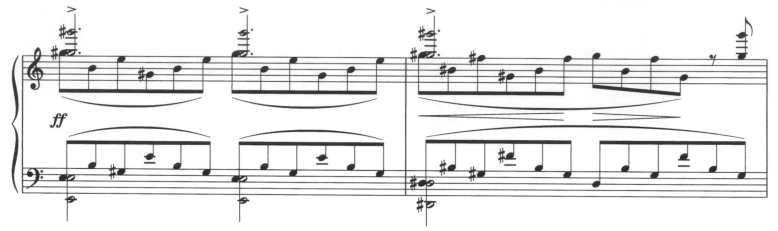

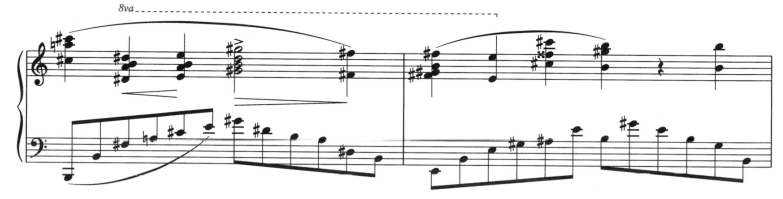

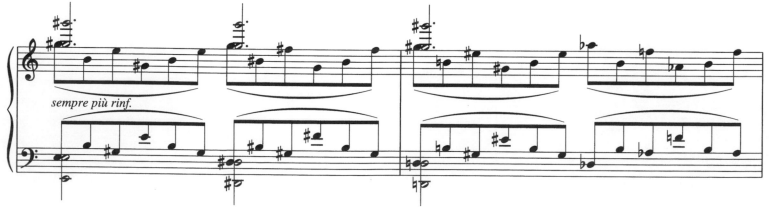

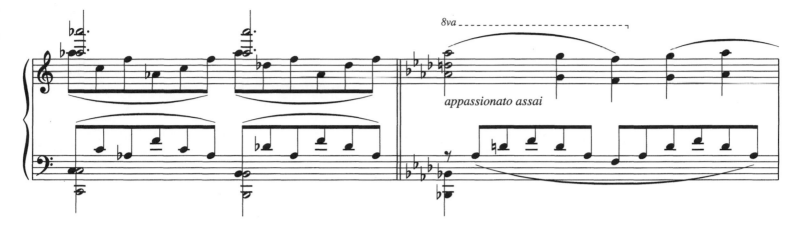

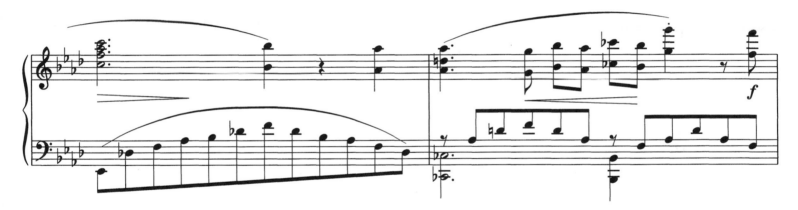

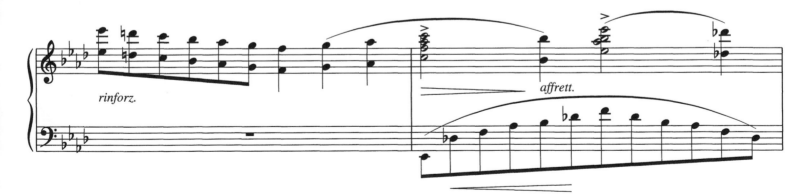

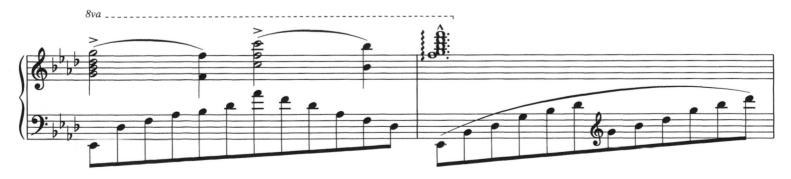

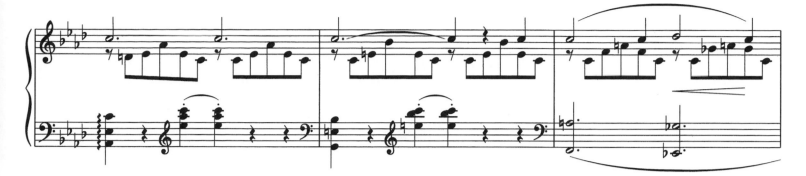

poco a poco riten.

più smorz. e rit.

Symphony No. 5 in C-sharp Minor

Fourth Movement Excerpt, "Adagietto"

Gustav Mahler
1860-1911
this movement originally
for strings and harp

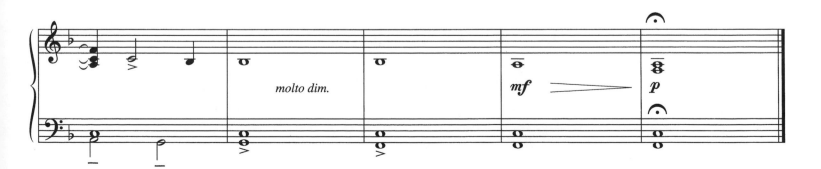

Symphony No. 8 in E Major
"Symphony of a Thousand"
Second Movement Excerpt, Orchestral Introduction to the Final Scene from FAUST

Gustav Mahler
1860-1911
originally for chorus, organ and orchestra

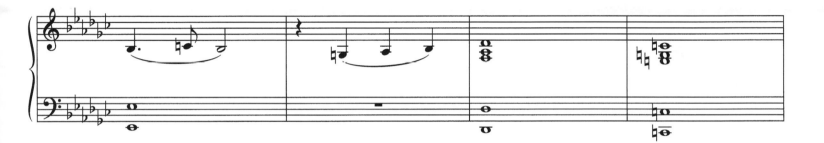

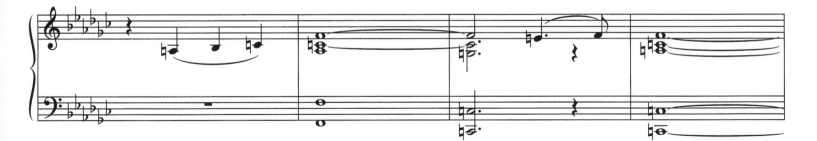

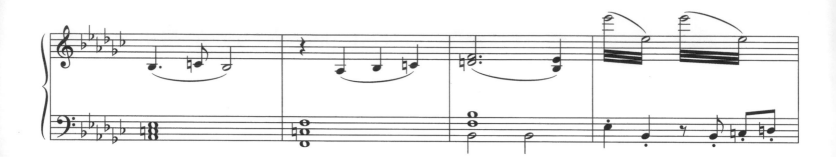

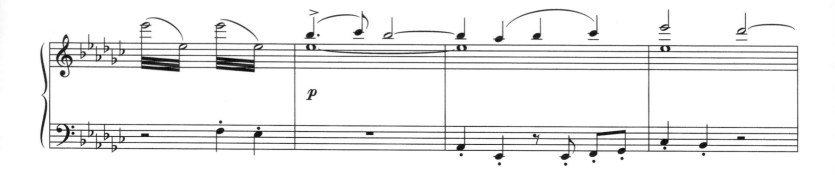

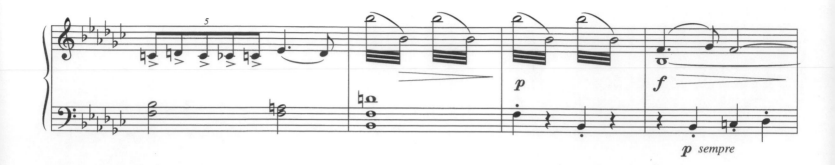

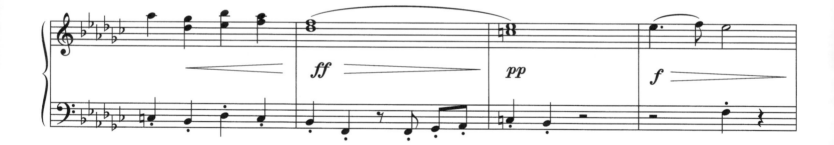

Meditation
from the opera THAÏS

Jules Massenet
1842–1912

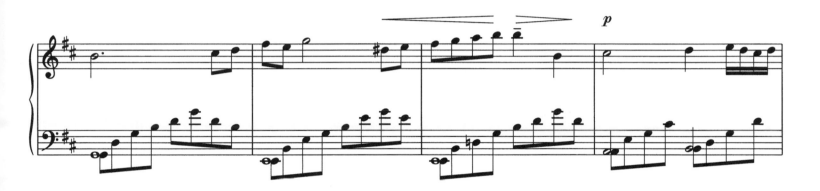

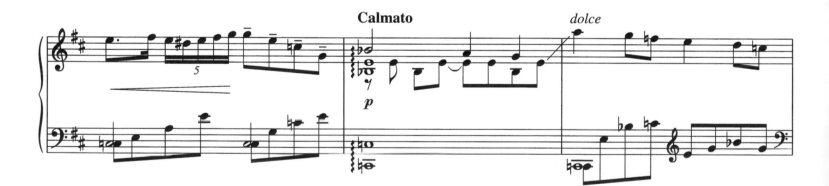

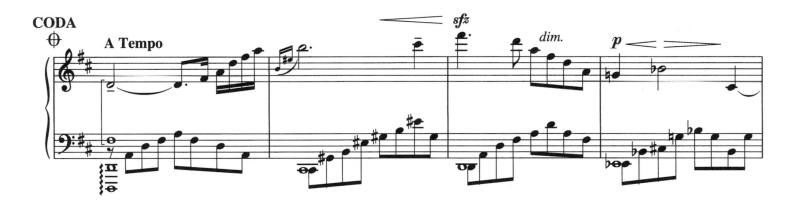

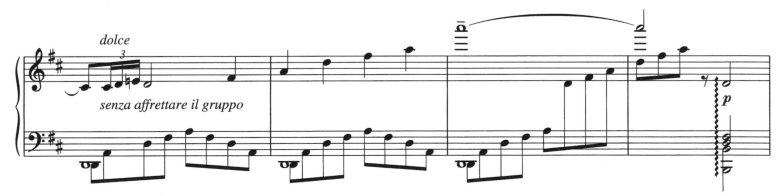

"Fingal's Cave" Overture

or "The Hebrides"
Themes

Felix Mendelssohn
1809-1847
Op. 26
originally for orchestra

Allegro moderato

Animato

A Midsummer Night's Dream

Overture Themes

Felix Mendelssohn
1809-1847
Op. 61
originally for orchestra

Allegro di molto

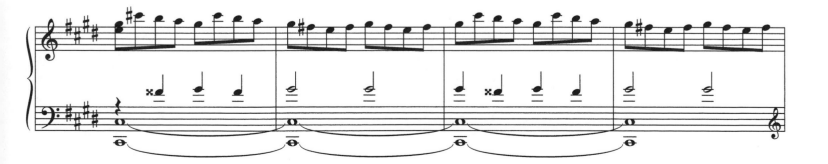

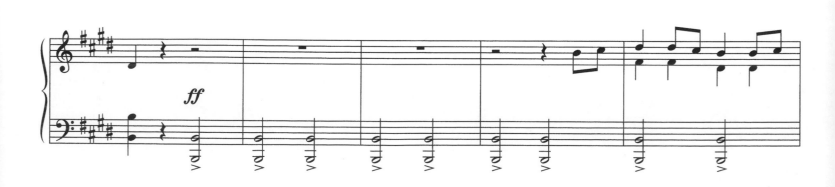

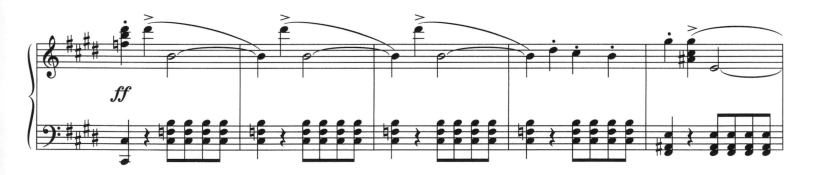

Symphony No. 4 in A Major

"Italian"
First Movement Excerpt

Felix Mendelssohn
1809-1847
Op. 90
originally for orchestra

Allegro vivace

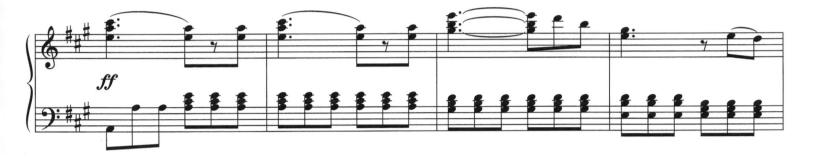

The Great Gate of Kiev
from PICTURES AT AN EXHIBITION

Modest Musorgsky
1839–1881

Allegro alla breve
Maestoso con grandezza

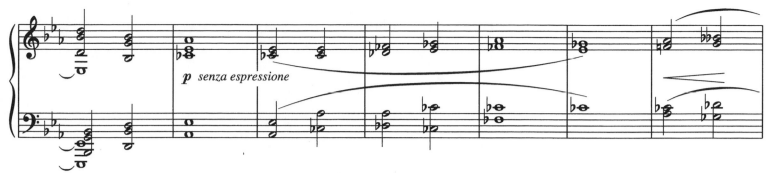

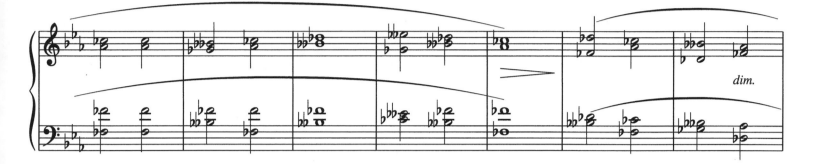

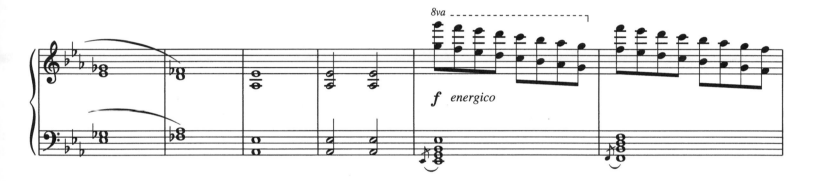

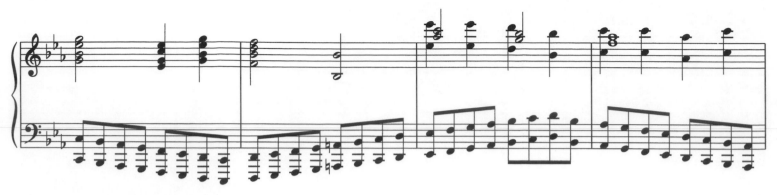

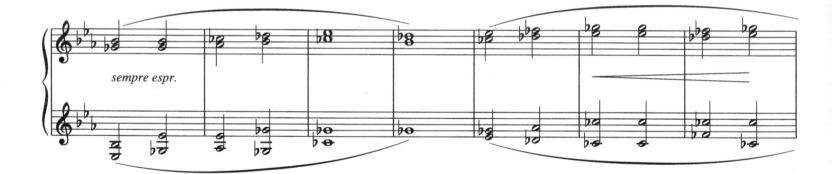

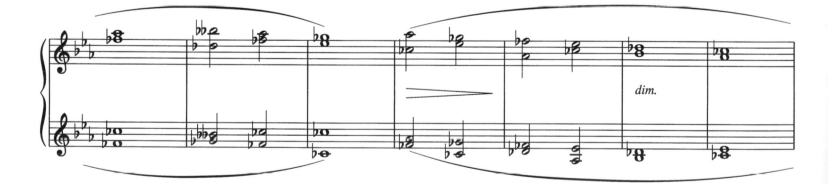

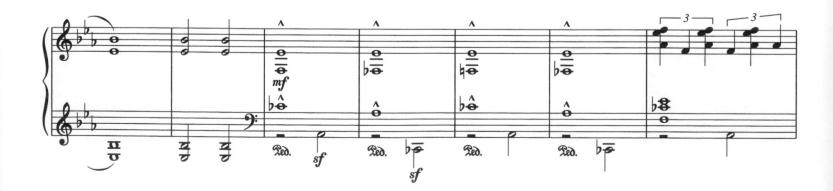

Meno mosso e sempre maestoso

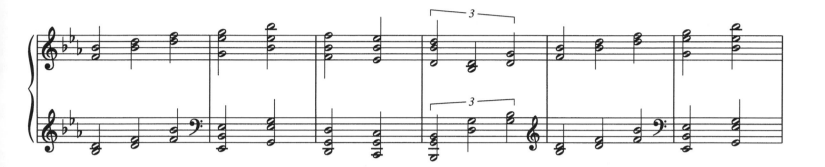

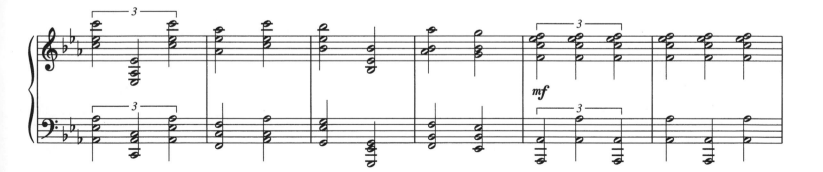

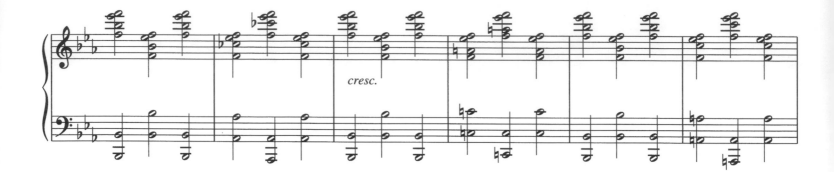

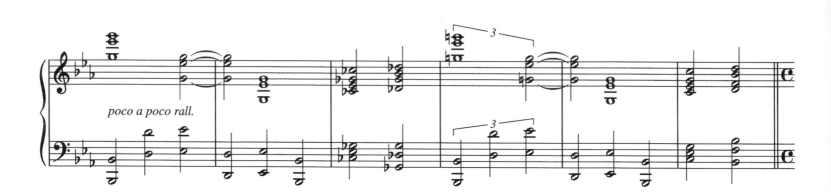

Grave sempre allargando

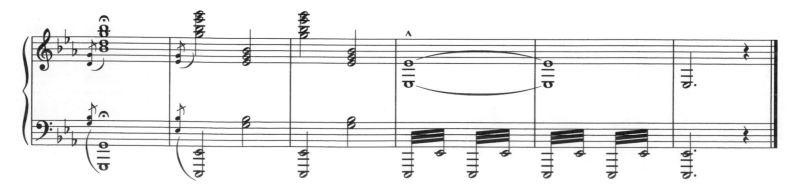

Barcarolle

from the opera LES CONTES D'HOFFMANN
(The Tales of Hoffmann)

Jacques Offenbach
1819–1880

sempre più dolce

morendo

ppp

Prelude in C-sharp Minor

Sergei Rachmaninoff
1873-1943
Op. 3, No. 2

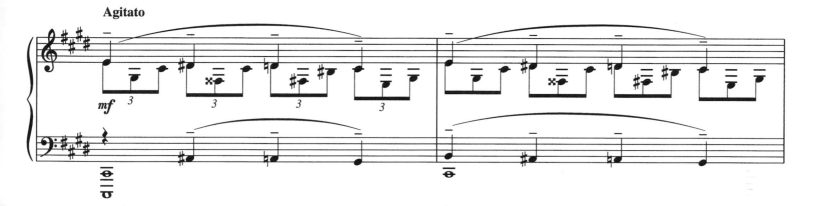

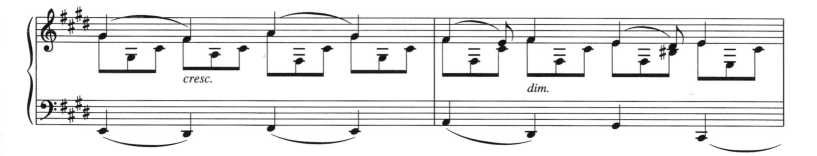

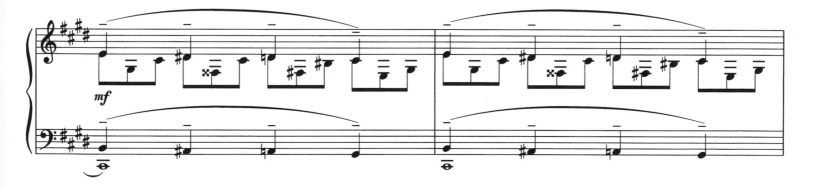

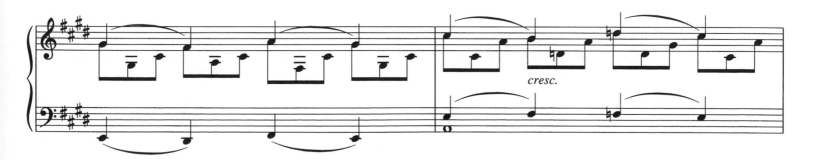

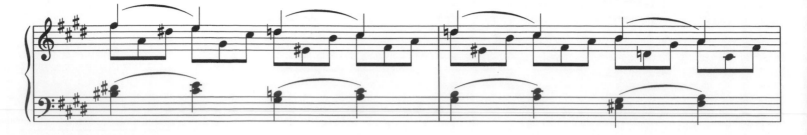

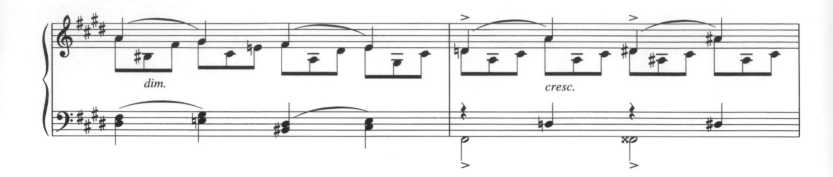

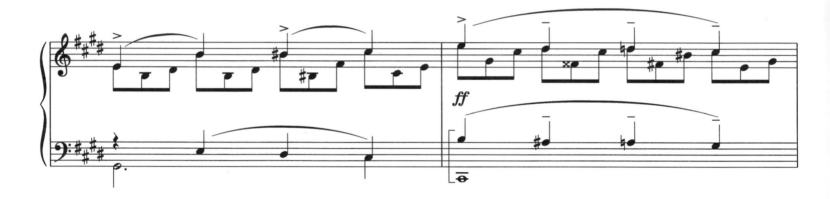

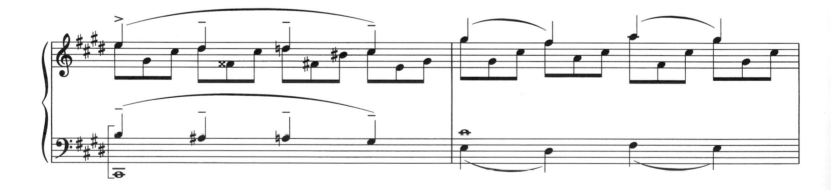

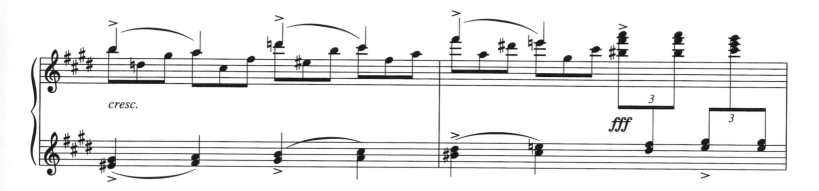

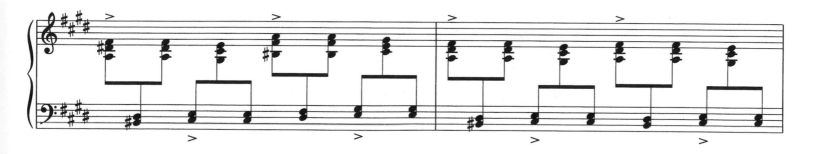

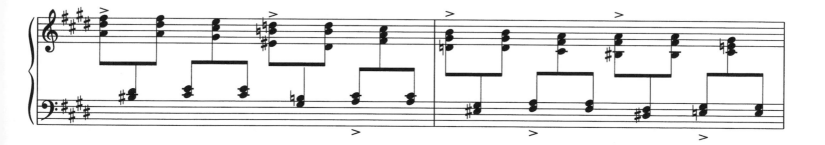

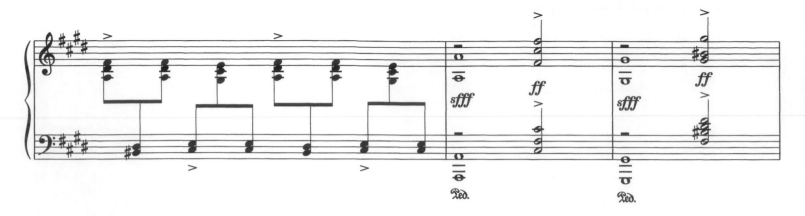

Tempo I

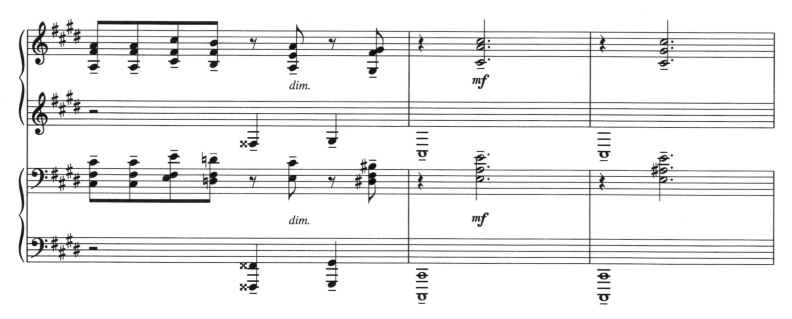

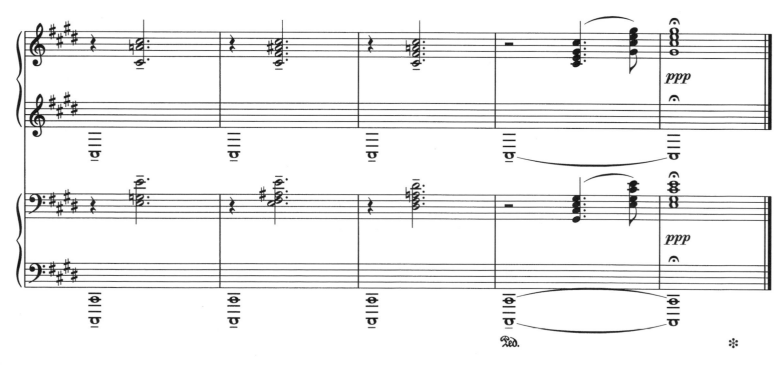

Andante
(Second Movement)
from SONATA IN A MAJOR

Franz Schubert
1797-1828
Op. 120 (D. 664)

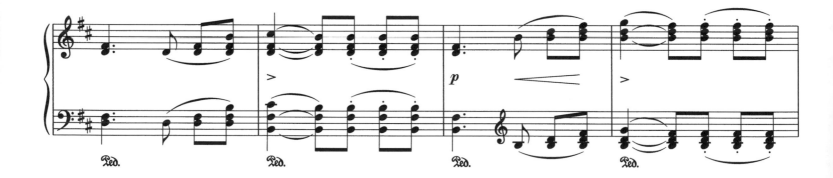

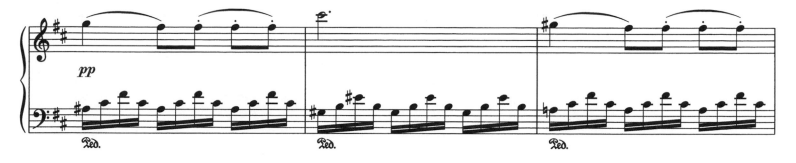

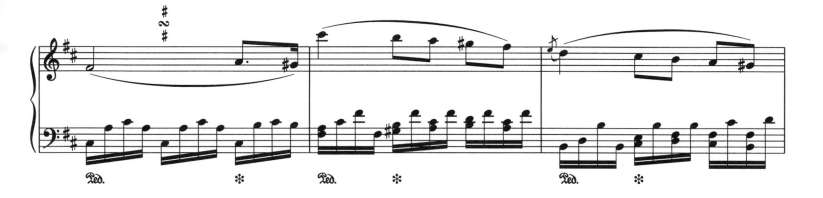

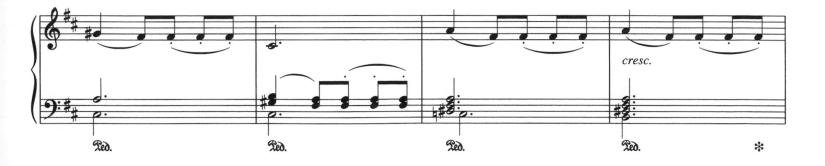

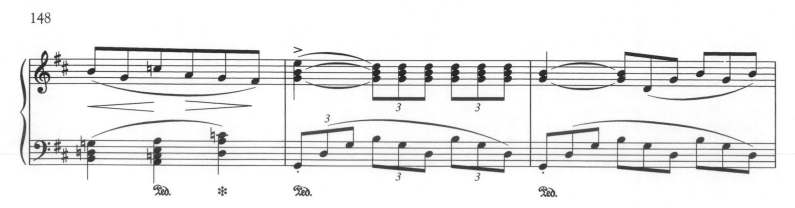

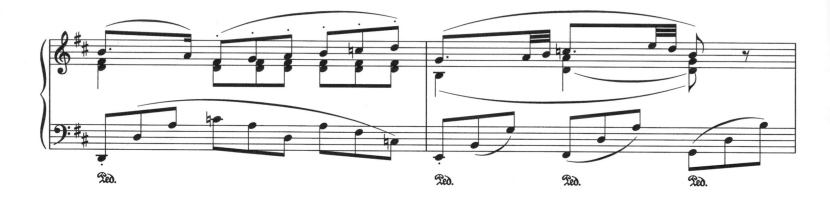

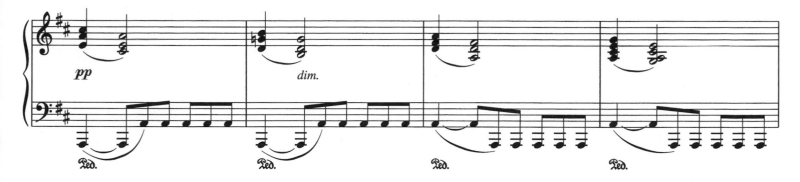

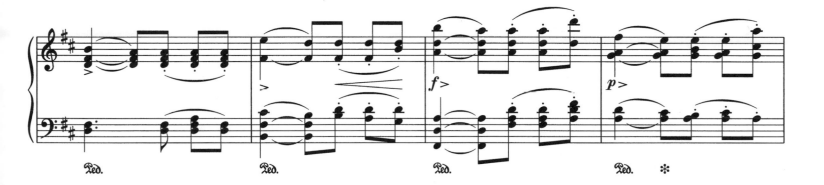

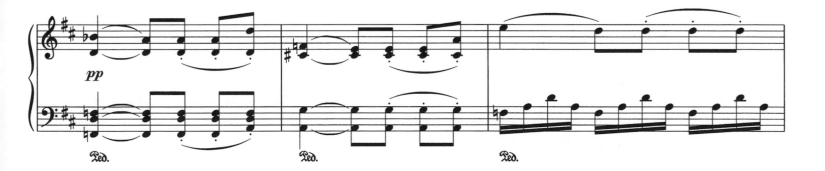

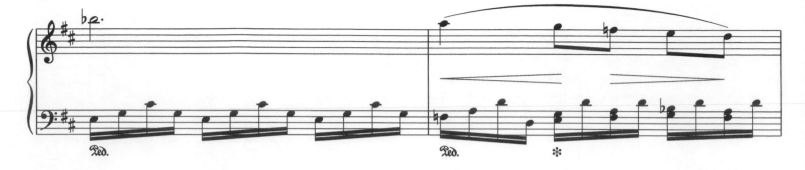

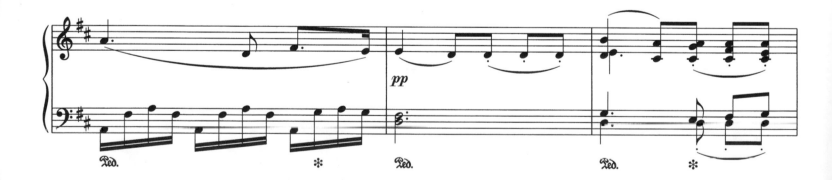

Sheherazade
Themes from Part 1

Nikolay Andreyevich Rimsky-Korsakov
1844-1908
Op. 35
originally for orchestra

Allegro non troppo

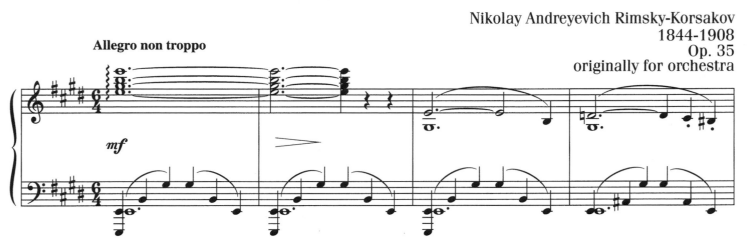

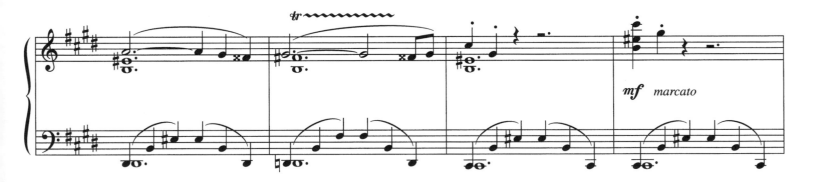

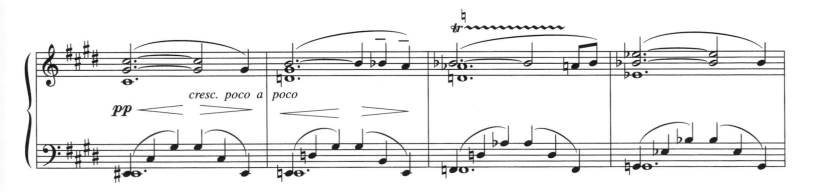

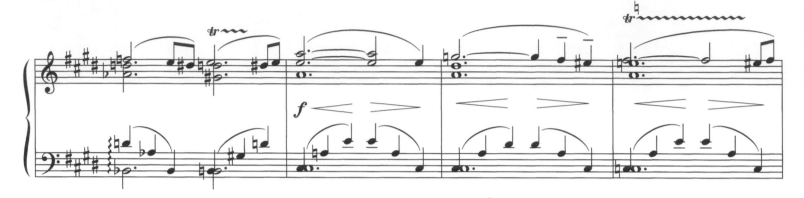

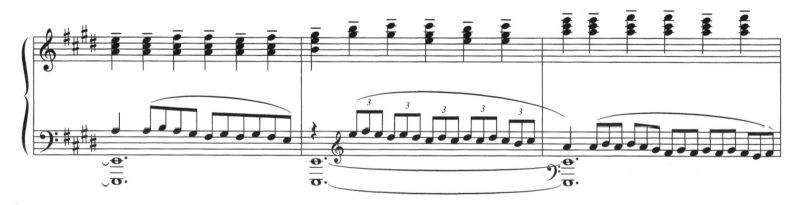

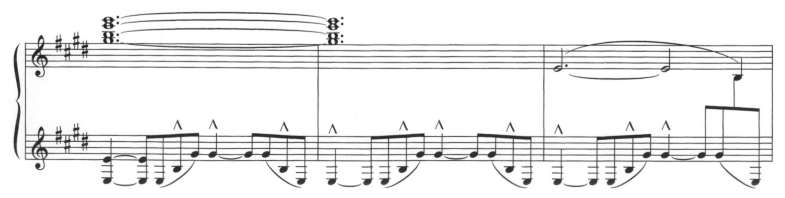

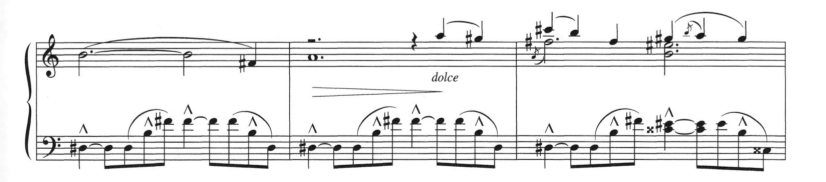

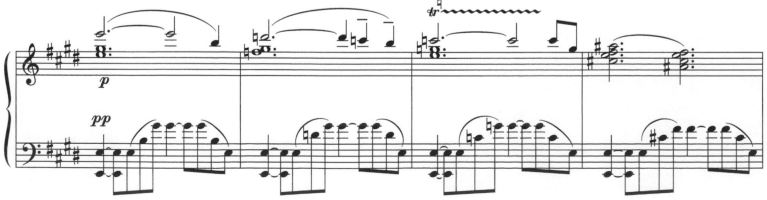

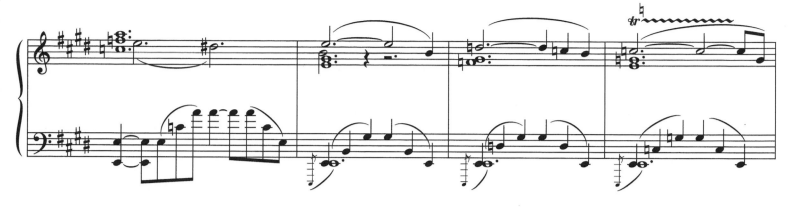

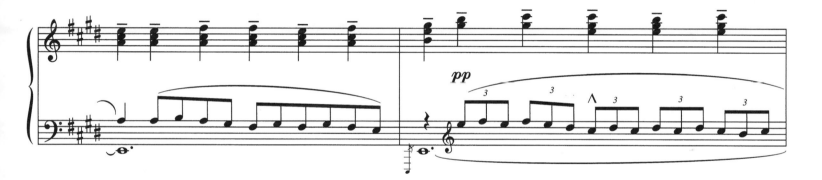

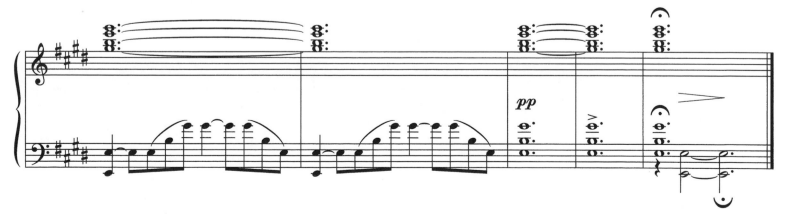

Ave Maria

Franz Schubert
1797-1828
D. 839
originally for voice and piano

Molto lento

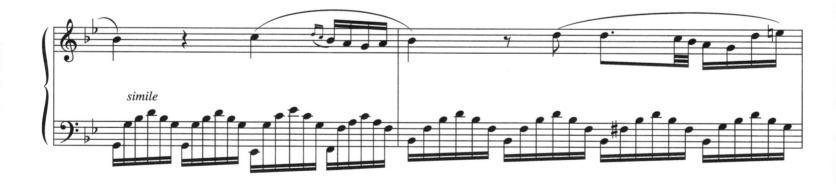

Piano Concerto in A Minor
First Movement Themes

Robert Schumann
1810-1856
Op. 54
originally for piano and orchestra

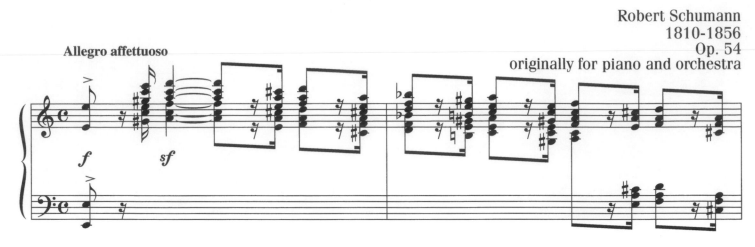

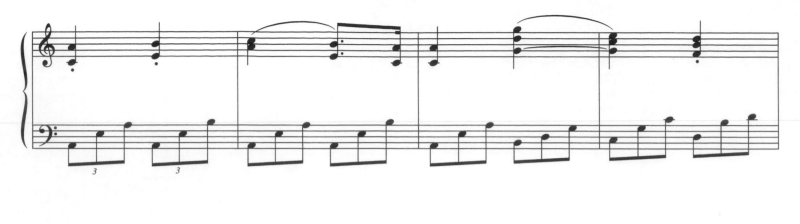

Impromptu in A-flat Major

Franz Schubert
1797-1828
Op. 142, No.2 (D. 935)

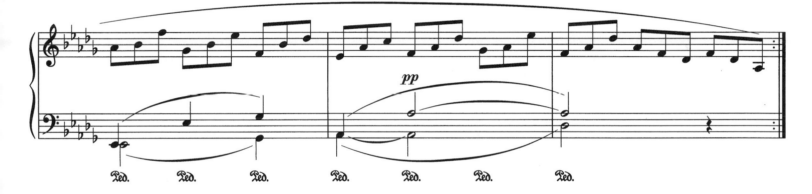

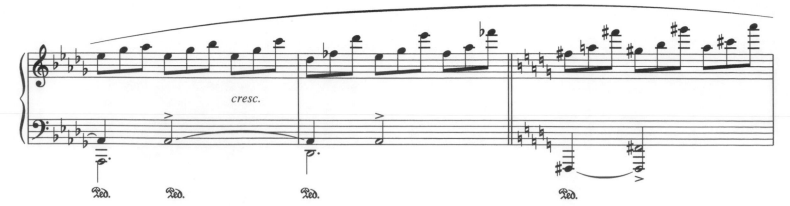

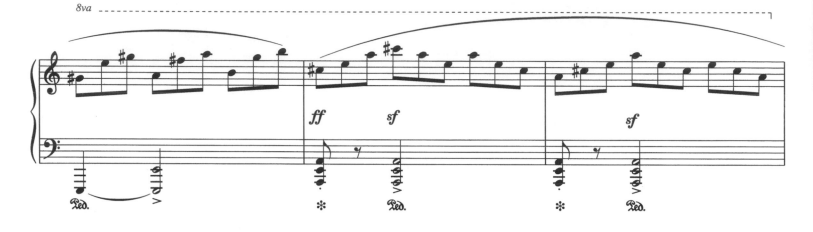

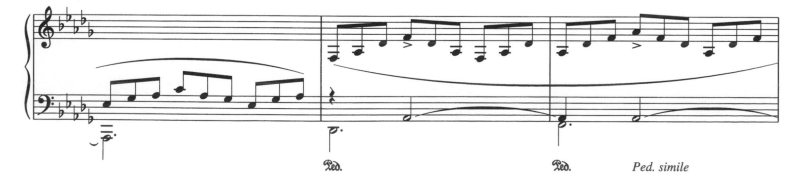

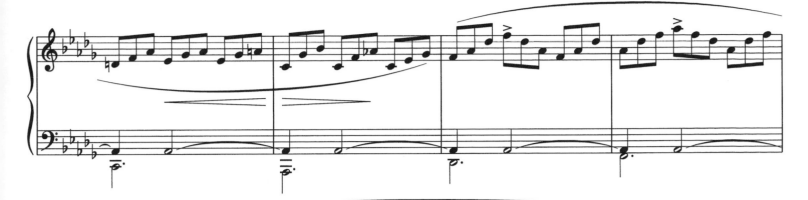

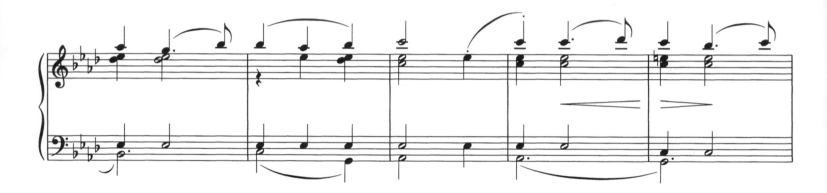

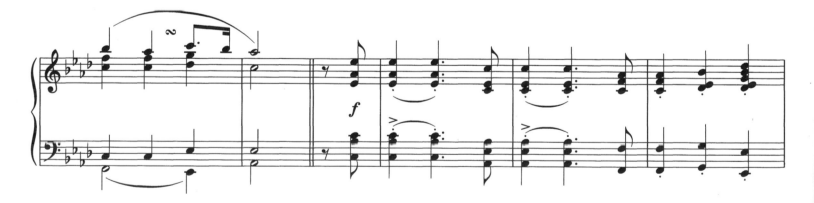

Moment Musicale in F Minor

Franz Schubert
1797–1828
D. 780, No. 5 (Op. 94, No. 5)

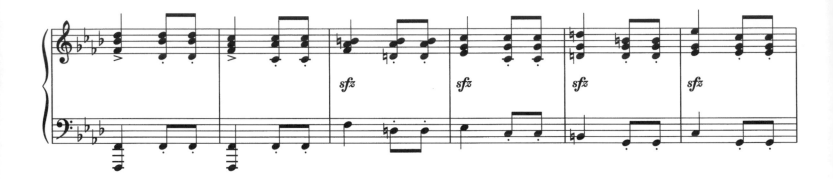

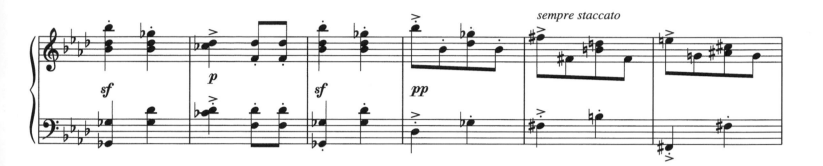

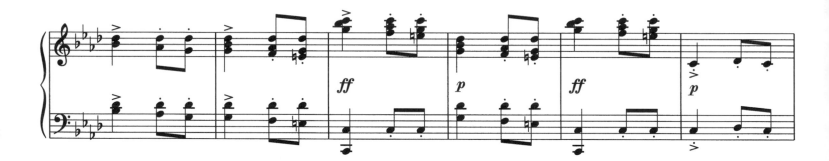

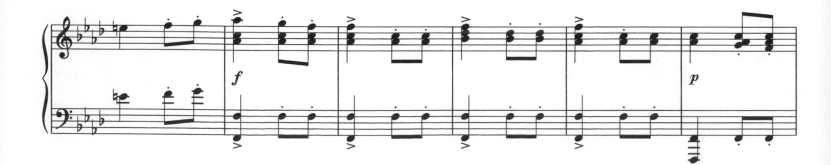

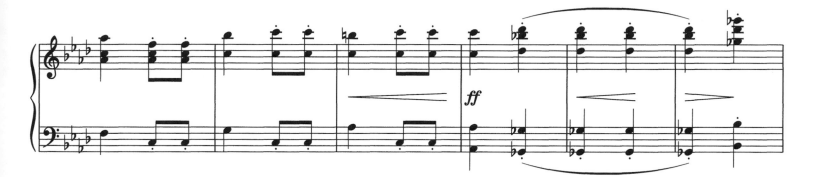

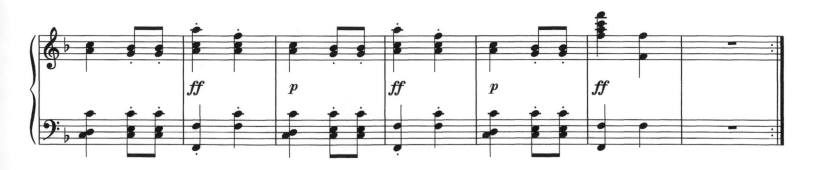

Symphony No. 8 in B minor

"Unfinished"

First Movement Excerpt

Franz Schubert
1797-1828
D. 759
originally for orchestra

Allegro moderato

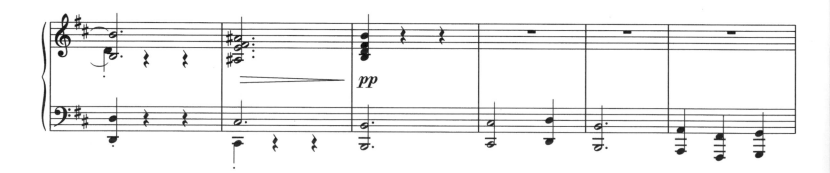

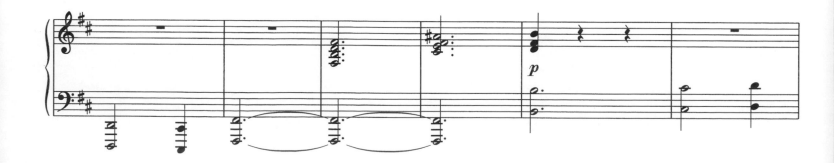

Symphony No. 9 in C Major
"The Great"
First Movement Excerpt

Franz Schubert
1797-1828
D. 944
published posthumously
originally for orchestra

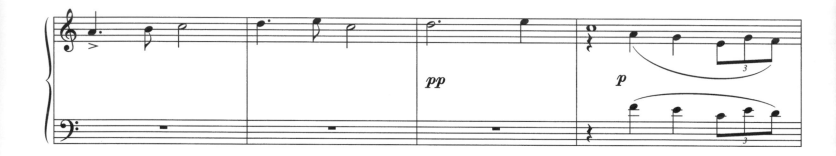

The Prophet Bird
(Vogel als Prophet)
from WALDSCENEN
(Forest Scenes)

Robert Schumann
1810-1856
Op. 82

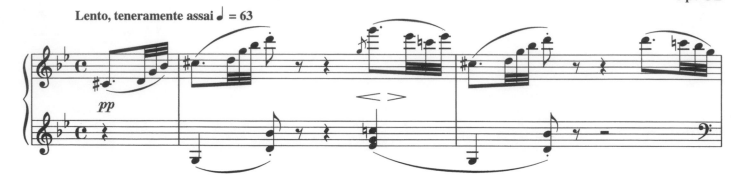

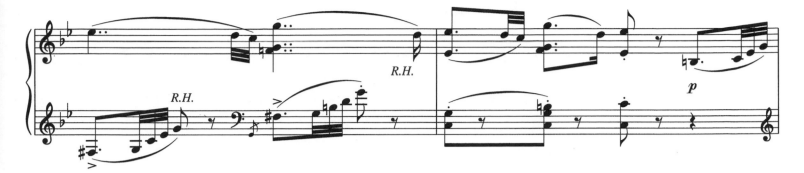

184

Un poco più lento

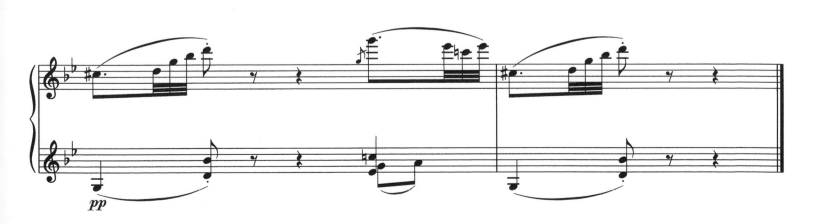

Symphony No. 1 in B-flat Major

"Spring"
Third Movement Excerpt, "Scherzo"

Robert Schumann
1810-1856
Op. 38
originally for orchestra

Molto vivace

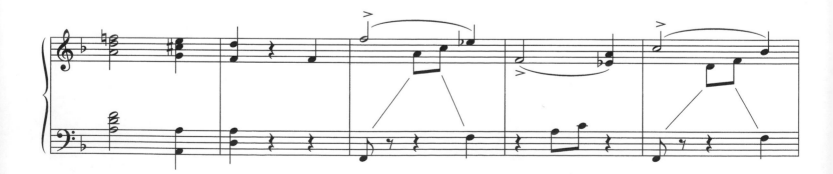

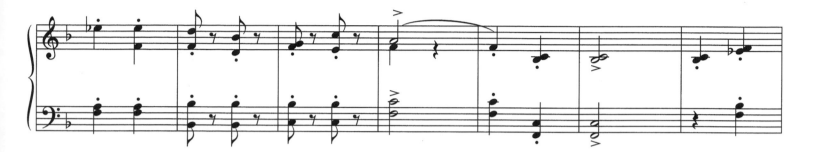

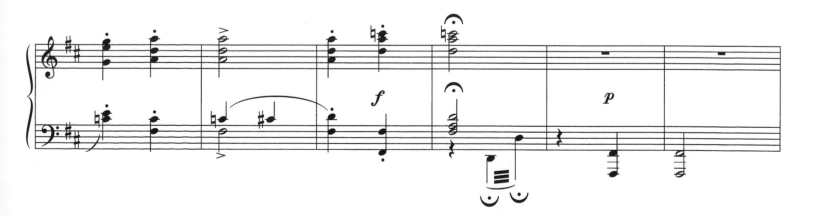

By the Beautiful Blue Danube

Themes

Johann Strauss Jr.
1825-1899
Op. 317
originally for orchestra

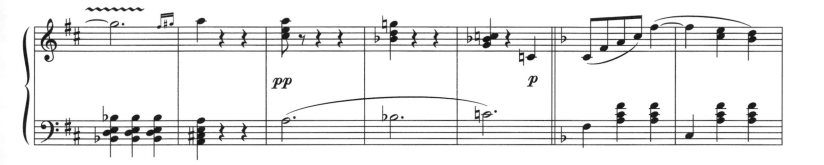

Widmung
(Dedication)

Robert Schumann
1810–1856
Op. 25, No. 1
originally for voice and piano

Innig, lebhaft

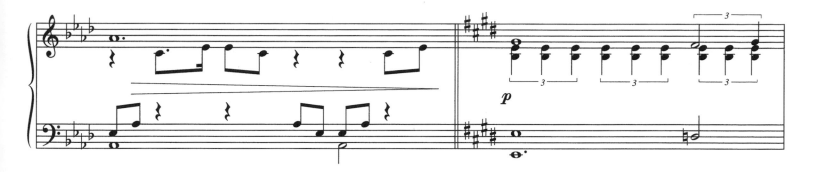

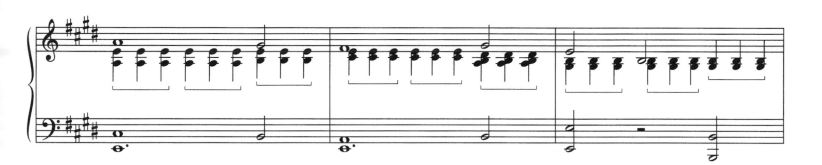

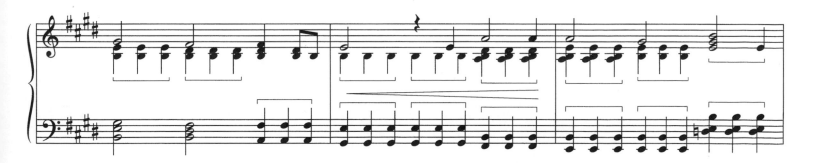

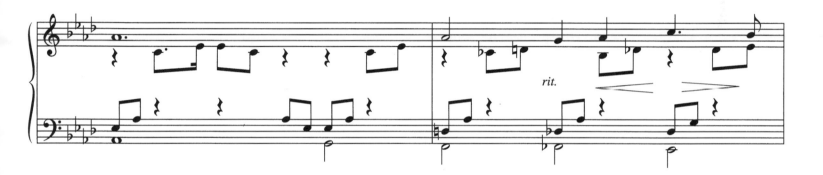

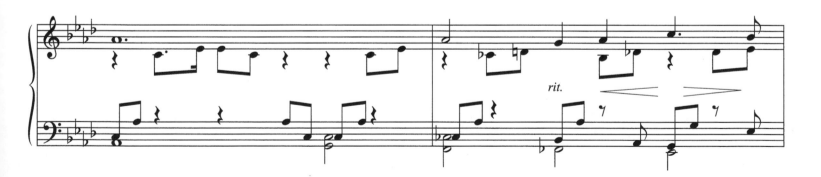

Tales from the Vienna Woods

Themes

Johann Strauss Jr.
1825-1899
Op. 325
originally for orchestra

Tempo di Valse

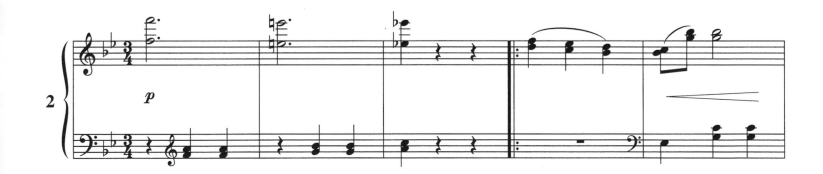

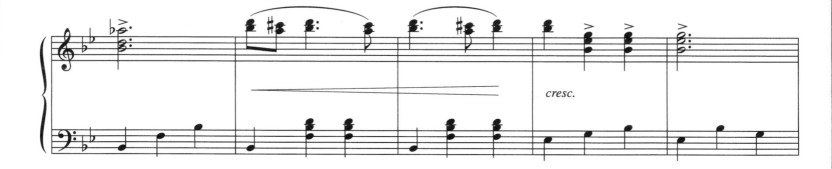

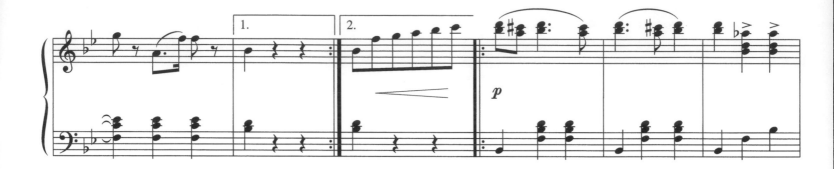

Allerseelen
(All Souls' Day)

Richard Strauss
1864-1949
Op. 10, No. 8
originally for voice and piano

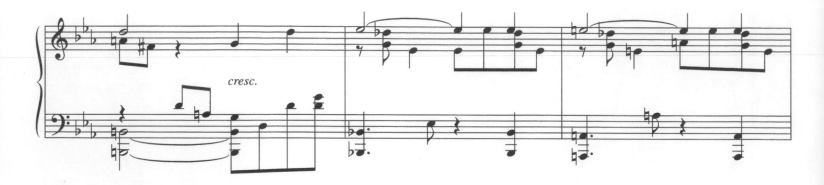

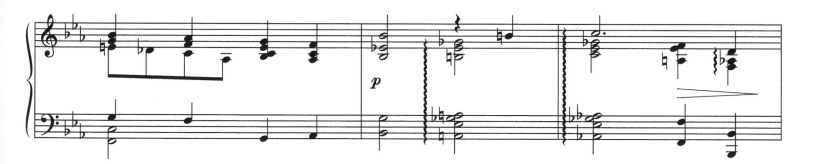

1812 Overture
Excerpt

Pyotr Il'yich Tchaikovsky
1840-1893
Op. 49
originally for orchestra

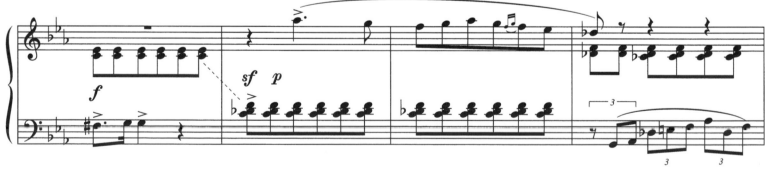

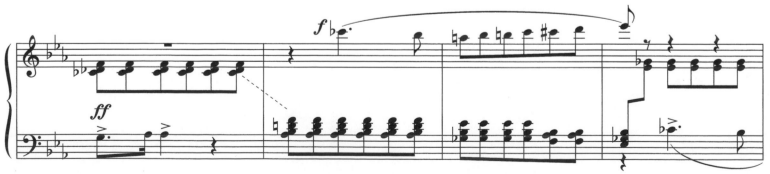

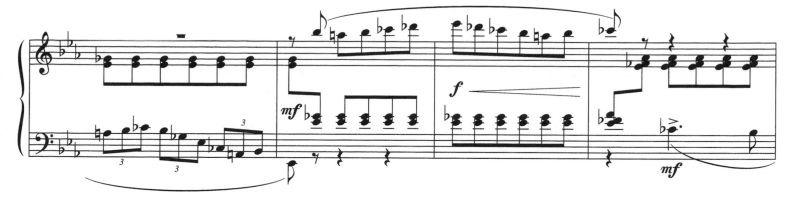

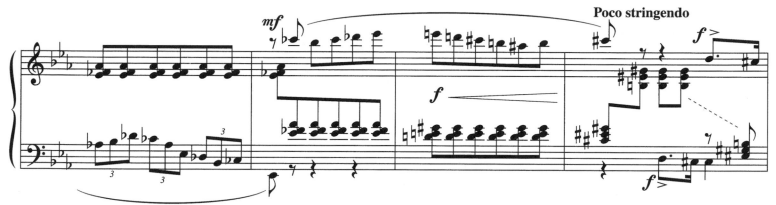

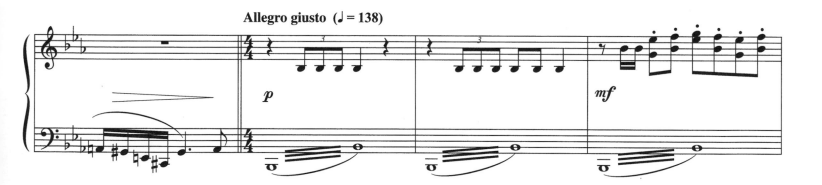

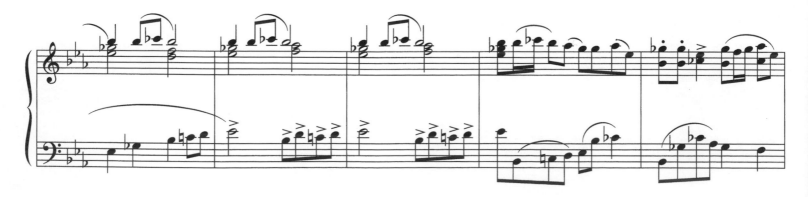

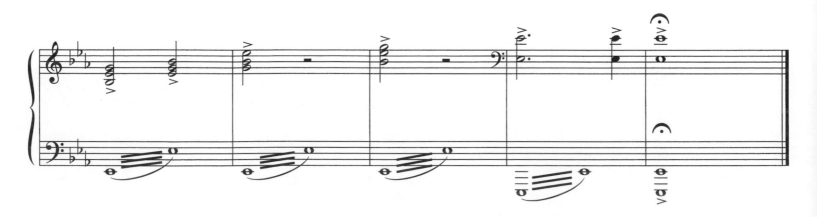

Also Sprach Zarathustra!
Opening Theme

Richard Strauss
1864-1949
Op. 30
originally for orchestra

Dance of the Sugar Plum Fairy
from the ballet THE NUTCRACKER

Pyotr Il'yich Tchaikovsky
1840–1893
Op. 71
originally for orchestra

Andante ma non troppo

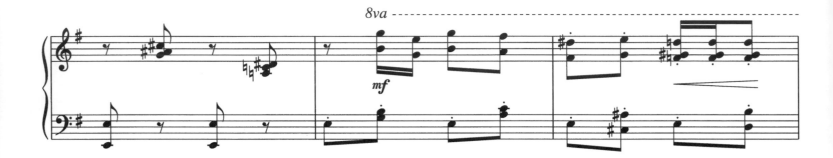

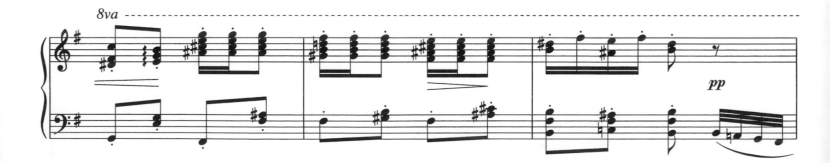

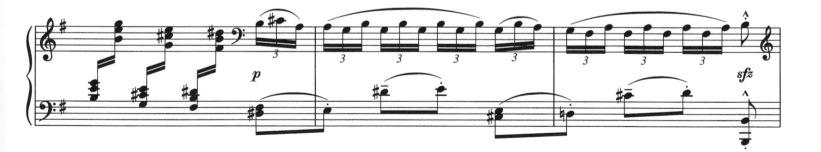

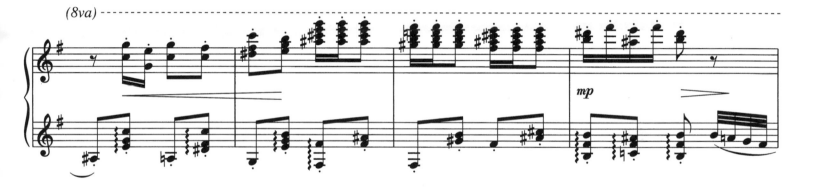

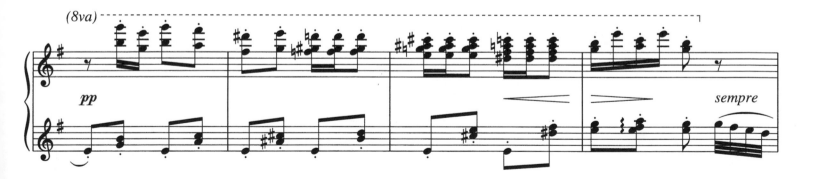

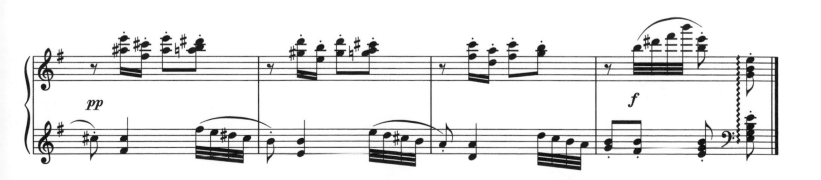

Piano Concerto No. 1 in B-flat Minor
First Movement Excerpt

Pyotr Il'yich Tchaikovsky
1840-1893
Op. 23
originally for piano and orchestra

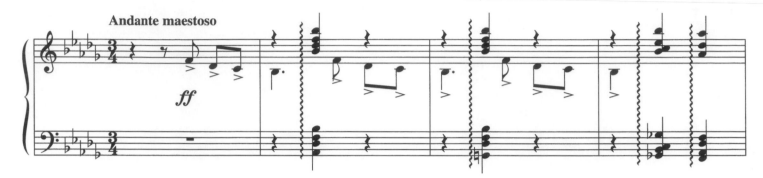

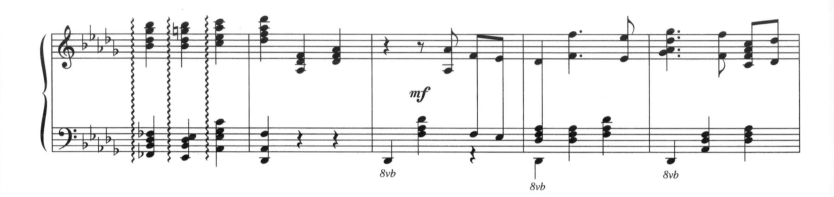

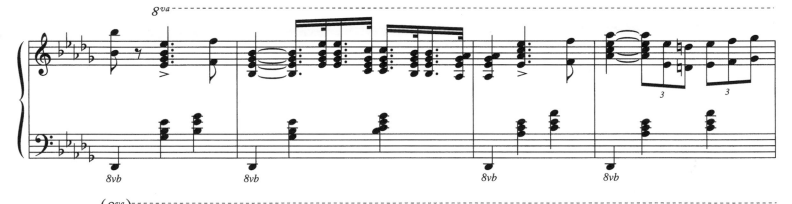

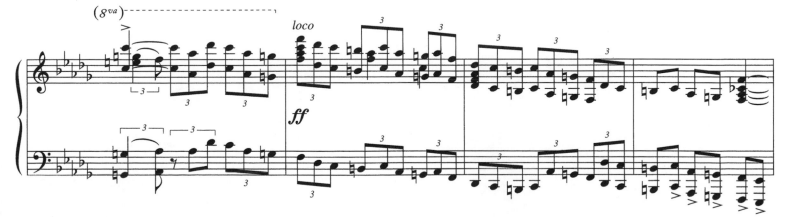

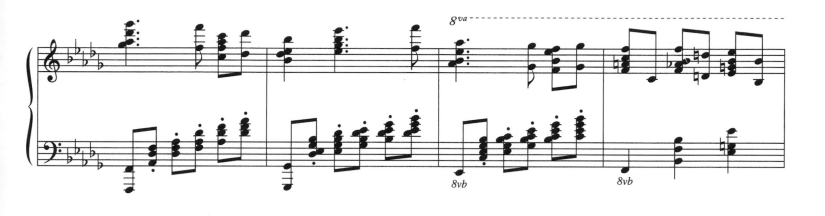

Romeo and Juliet

Fantasy Overture

"Love Theme"

Pyotr Il'yich Tchaikovsky
1840-1893
originally for orchestra

Allegro giusto

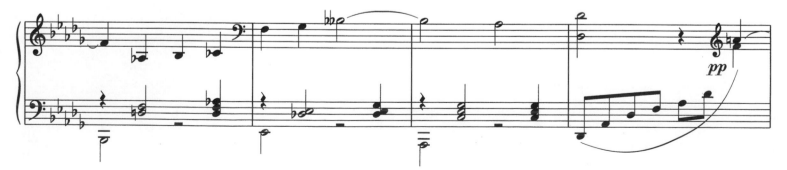

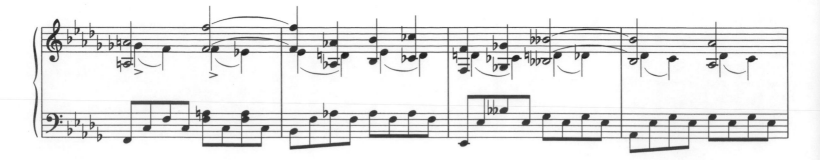

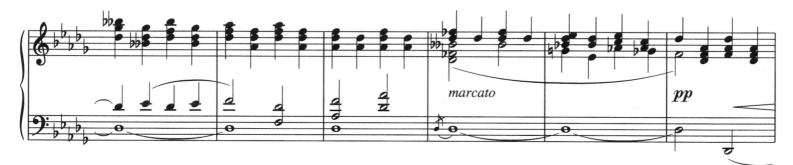

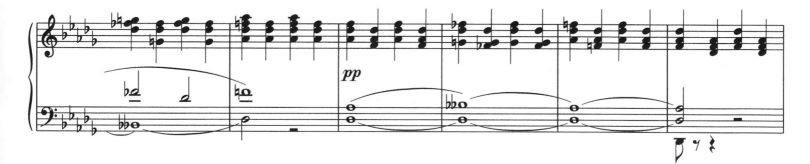

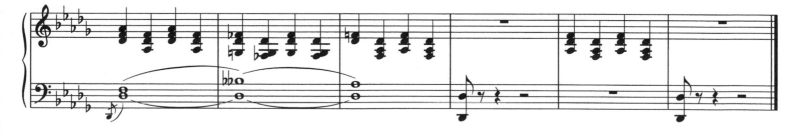

Symphony No. 6 in B Minor

"Pathétique"
First Movement Excerpt

Pyotr Il'yich Tchaikovsky
1840-1893
Op. 74
originally for orchestra

veneramente, molto cantabile con espressione

Adagio mosso

Andante mosso

Waltz of the Flowers

from the ballet THE NUTCRACKER

Excerpt

Pyotr Il'yich Tchaikovsky
1840-1893
Op. 71
originally for orchestra

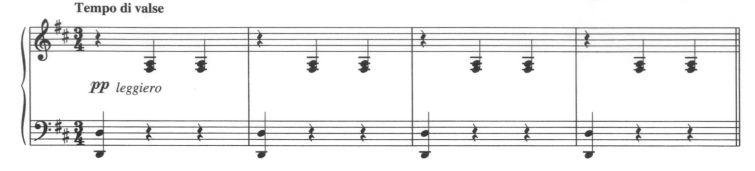

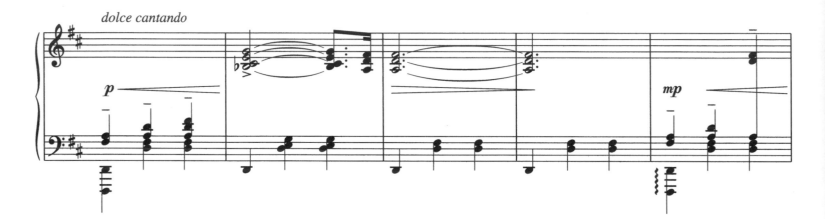

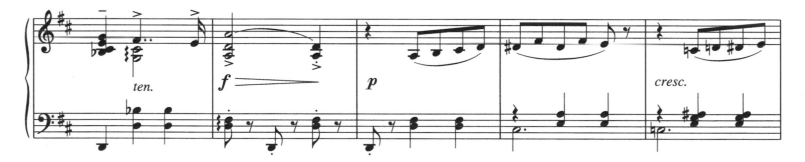

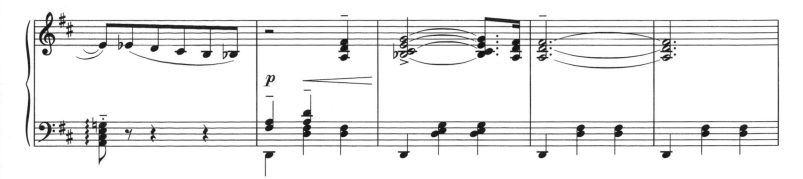

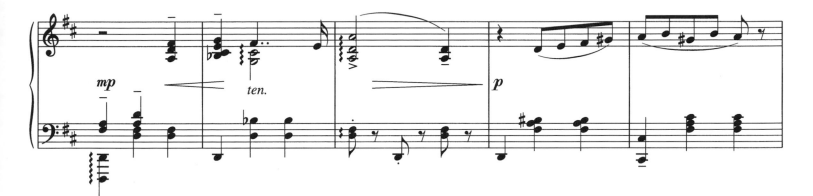

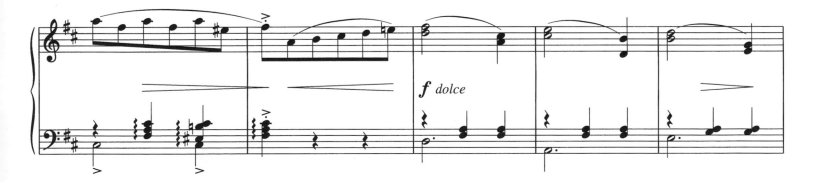

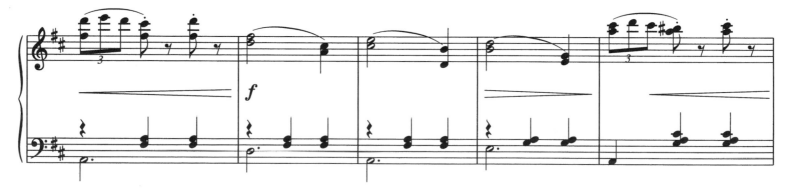

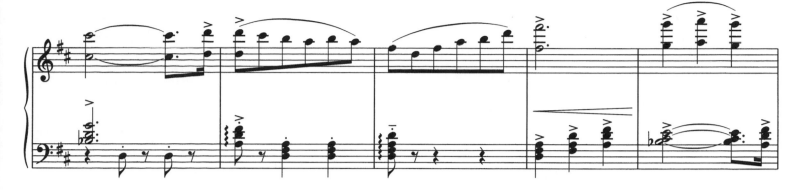

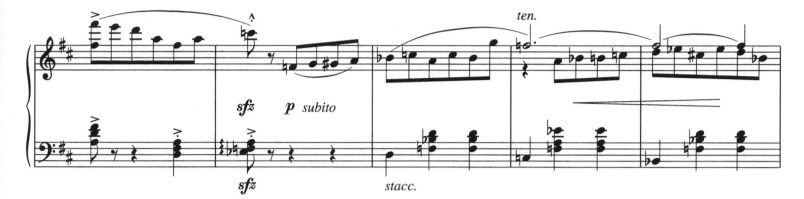

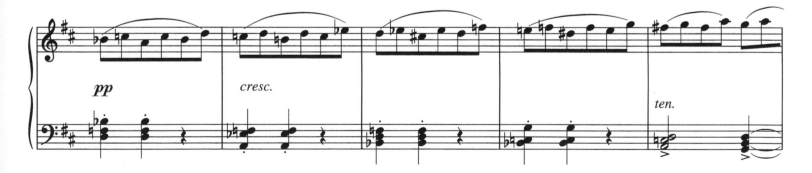

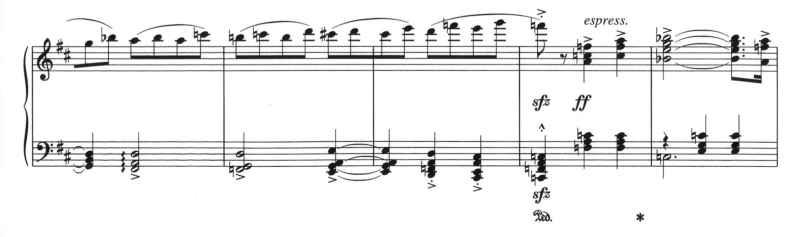

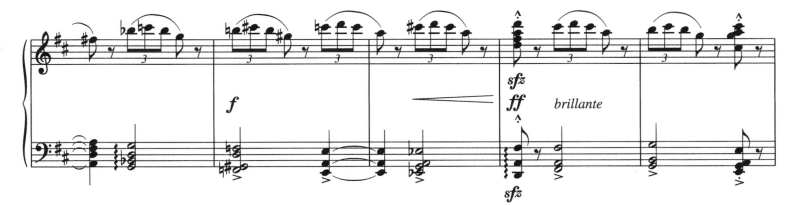

The Evening Star
TANNHÄUSER

Richard Wagner
1813-1883

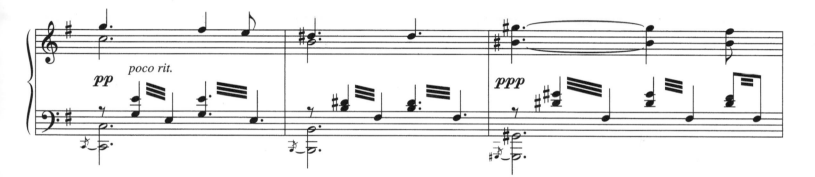

Pilgrims' Chorus
from the opera TANNHÄUSER

Richard Wagner
1813-1883
originally for orchestra

Andante maestoso

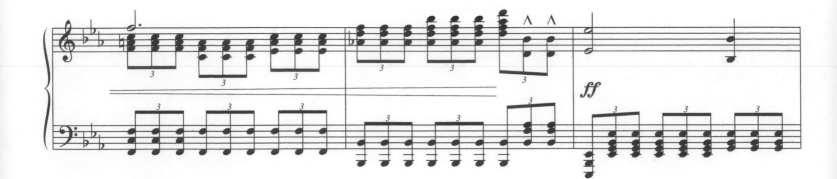

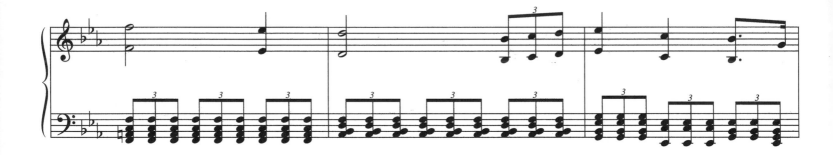

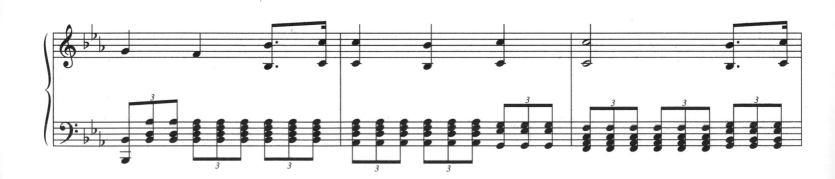

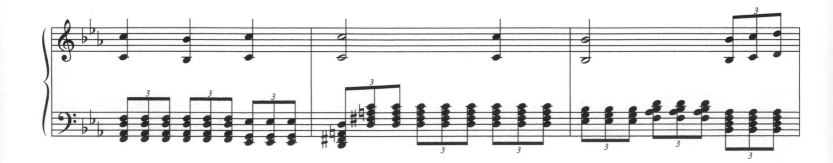

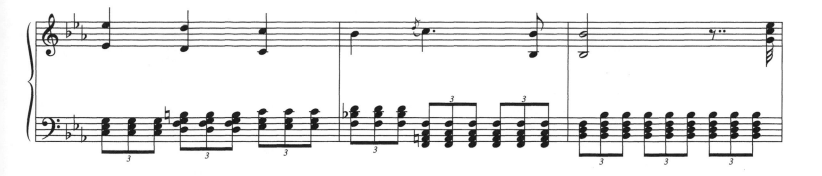

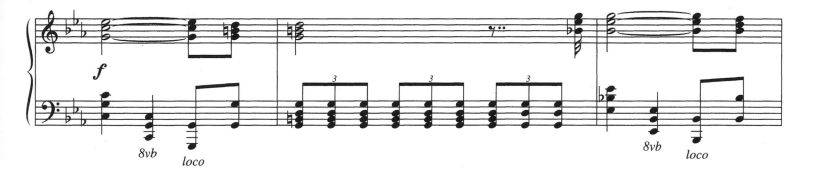

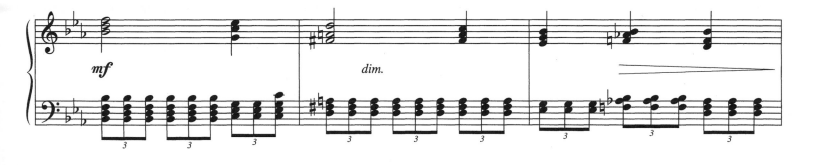

Waltz
from the ballet SWAN LAKE

Pyotr Il'yich Tchaikovsky
1840-1893
originally for orchestra

Tempo di Valse

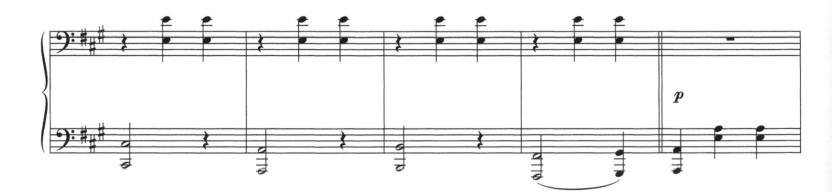

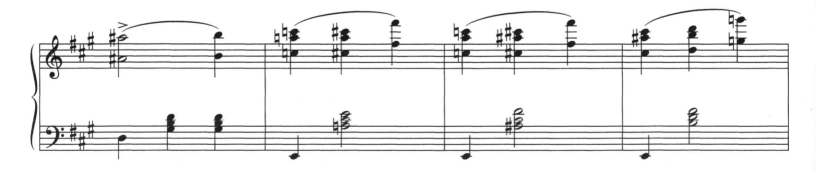